The Jazz Age

FISK TIRES

CHEVROLET
BUYING

By Marvin Barrett

PICTURE EDITOR:
William Cahn

THE

*Based on the N.B.C. Television
Project 20 Program "The Jazz Age,"
written by Henry Salomon with Richard Hanser*

JAZZ AGE

G. P. Putnam's Sons NEW YORK

A special acknowledgments section appears in the rear of this book.

Library of Congress Catalog Card Number: 59-11006
Manufactured in the United States of America

Contents

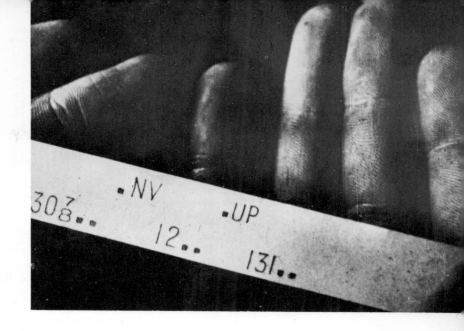

Introduction

The Jazz Age—1919 to 1929—ten years out of a nation's young life. What does it amount to? A little, and a lot. In 1919 the United States has had nearly a century and a half to grow. It has been initiated into the company of adult nations by a great war. The cost: 338 billion dollars squandered; ten million dead. With a youth's candor, arrogance, and capacity for violent disillusion a country draws back from the claims of maturity into a short, wild adolescence. It lasts precisely a decade; a decade that is hilarious and vicious, productive and destructive, ultimately exhausting. The Roaring Twenties, The Age of Confusion, The Gaudiest Spree in History, The Golden Boom, the Age of Wonderful Nonsense, The Lawless Decade—The Jazz Age—its very nicknames are emphatic and contradictory.

How did it all begin?

The Beginning

It begins with Woodrow Wilson at Versailles . . . an idealist among cynics at the grandest palace in the world. Louis XIV started to build its glittering halls about the same time the French began to do the Minuet. Since then this château to end all châteaux has seen Empires rise and fall, monarchs come and go, a dozen dances fade from fashion. And now in 1919, its mirrors are about to reflect still another change.

The war is over. The capitals of the world have celebrated its end. In New York, undergraduates at Barnard College have snake-danced on Morningside Heights and a girl in white has sung the Doxology in Times Square. In Hell's Kitchen the Kaiser has been burned in effigy for the final time.

Woodrow Wilson has declared "everything for which America fought has been accomplished." Now he has to prove it.

The descendants of the men and women who marched out from Paris to Versailles in anger to grab Louis the Sixteenth and Marie Antoinette rush out in joy to hail "Mees-

November 11, 1918,
New York City

Johnny Comes
Marching Home

3

ter Veelson" and the twentieth-century peacemakers.

Peacemakers?

Clemenceau of France, "The Tiger," the champion of Dreyfus, the defender of justice, now a belligerent and vigorous seventy-eight, declares, "The greater the sanguinary catastrophe which devastated and ruined the richest regions of France, the more ample and splendid shall be the reparations." He sneers at Wilson's noble, self-effacing Fourteen Points. "Wilson has Fourteen; the Good Lord himself had only Ten. Mr. Wilson has lived in a world that has been fairly safe for democracy; I have lived in a world where it was good form to shoot a democrat." Witty, intransigent, tough, Clemenceau gets enough of his way to make impossible Wilson's visionary "establishment of just democracy throughout the world."

"What am I to do between a man who thinks he is Jesus Christ and another who thinks he is Napoleon?" is the contribution of Britain's Lloyd George, who has been launched from a "Hang the Kaiser" platform at home. Eventually when fisticuffs threaten, Peacemaker Wilson has to separate Clemenceau and George but he can't prevent another peacemaker, Orlando of Italy, from going home in a huff, because he isn't getting his way in Trieste, in the Trentino, in Dalmatia and Asia Minor.

"Everybody at the table wants a second helping, and Germany the cook hasn't enough to go around," cracks Will Rogers, a fancy rope artist in the *Ziegfeld Follies* who will become the Jazz Age's La Rochefoucauld.

Behind the noble façade of Right, Truth, Justice, Freedom, Democracy, the "self-determination of nations," no indemnities, no annexations, are the squalid realities—the Rhineland, Danzig, the starving Armenians, the Polish Corridor, Palestine, the Ruhr, the Saar, the Mespot, Transjordania, Shantung and the Island of Yap. In the Adriatic port of Fiume self-styled poet-hero Gabriele D'Annunzio lands with a private army in a spirited attempt to make life imitate his own flamboyant verse. If the peacemakers don't give us what we want, to hell with peace.

Clemenceau

Wilson, the dreamer, is no schemer.

"He had no plan," is the judgment of the eminent British Economist Maynard Keynes, "no scheme, no constructive ideas whatever for clothing with the flesh of life the commandments which he had thundered from the White House. He could have preached a sermon on any of them or have addressed a stately prayer to the Almighty for their fulfillment; but he could not frame their concrete application to the actual state of Europe."

One by one the Fourteen Points disappear into the mist of endless negotiations. "The self-determination of nations" deteriorates into a carving bee. "No indemnities" becomes meaningless when the first installment of German reparations is put at five billions with no limit to future payments indicated. Only the Covenant of the League of Nations remains—the Covenant that will abolish war and settle disputes by law and reason. Through six long months of debate and intrigue and compromise Woodrow Wilson holds stubbornly to one of his dreams and the Covenant is written into the treaty.

On June 28, 1919, in the Hall of Mirrors the treaty is signed. Outside the French troops, foot and cavalry, in full dress stand magnificent guard. Wilson, Clemenceau and George, their work done, go into the sunshine arm in arm to watch Louis's shimmering fountains support a thousand deceptive rainbows. For the moment it seems that, after all, despite the patching and the scratching, the problems of the world may be solved and its peaceful future insured.

While Wilson is fighting desperately for his own, and what he assumes are his countrymen's, ideals in Paris and Versailles, a "little group of willful men" in Washington are hard at work to make sure that what little he has accomplished will come to nought.

Their leader is the impressive, patrician gentleman from Massachusetts, Henry Cabot Lodge, enthusiastically aided and abetted by a couple of weighty senatorial confreres, Borah of Idaho and Johnson of California. To them Wil-

Orlando

5

The Hall of Mirrors

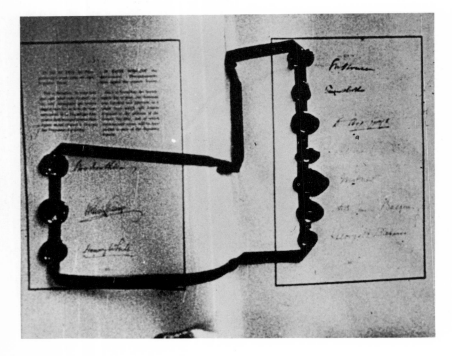

Pages from the Versailles Treaty

son's League of Nations looks like just another "foreign entanglement," another European trap laid for innocent Americans.

Wilson's answer to their growing voice is to go back to the people. While Lodge's Committee on Foreign Relations thumbs through his treaty in Washington, Wilson, against his doctor's orders, sets off across the country.

Forty hour-long speeches in 22 days, all different, all delivered in his quiet, gracefully incisive voice with its hint

The Big Four

The Fountains of Versailles

Borah and Johnson

Wilson in Triumph

8

of a Southern accent, all informed with a high purpose that sounds less compelling now that the war to keep the world safe for democracy is safely concluded. Eight thousand miles by special train.

"The affairs of America are linked to the affairs of men everywhere," Wilson pleads. "The hearts of men like Clemenceau and Lloyd George and Orlando beat with the people of the world," he rationalizes. His antagonists of Versailles have become benefactors now that he faces his American foes.

"See how the whole world turns with outstretched hands to this blessed country of ours and says, 'If you lead, we will follow.' God helping us, we will lead. . . . Dare we reject this treaty and break the heart of the world?"

"Yes," answers the voice of caution and disenchantment as the Senate votes against the President and the treaty.

"Now that the mists of this great question have cleared away, I believe that men will see the Truth eye for eye and face to face," reiterates the determined President, gray-faced with fatigue and disappointment, in Pueblo, Colorado. "There is one thing the American People always rise to and extend their hand to, that is, the truth of justice and of liberty and of peace. We have accepted that truth and we are going to be led by it, and it is going to lead us, and through us the world, out into pastures of quietness and peace such as the world never dreamed of before."

A few hours later Wilson collapses and his train turns back toward Washington.

"I have seen fools resist Providence before," he declares before his death four years later, "and I have seen their destruction, as will come upon these again—utter destruction and contempt. That we shall prevail is as sure as that God reigns."

But for the moment Wilson and Providence seem to be on the losing side. In the name of realism, responsibility is rejected, maturity delayed. It is time for the great spree to begin.

However, there is a slight delay.

Wilson in Defeat

League of Nations Great Britain will forthwith recognize the existence and political independence of the republic of Ireland and agree that it become a member of the League of Nations with equal representation accorded to all other sovereign and independent Governments.

Mr. THOMAS proposes to amend those words in four particulars so that, if amended, it will read:

The United States further understands that in fulfillment and execution of the great principle of self-determination of peoples and equality of all Governments pervading and underlying the covenant of the League of Nations Great Britain and Japan, respectively, will forthwith recognize the existence and political independence of the republic of Ireland and the ancient kingdom of Korea, and agree that they become members of the League of Nations with equal representation accorded to all other sovereign and independent Governments.

So that the reservation, if amended, will read:

The United States understands the protectorate referred to in section G of the treaty to have been merely a war measure to preserve the integrity and independence of Egypt during the war.

The United States further understands that in fulfillment and execution of the great principle of self-determination of peoples and equality of all Governments pervading and underlying the covenant of the League of Nations Great Britain and Japan, respectively, will forthwith recognize the existence and political independence of the republic of Ireland and the ancient kingdom of Korea, and agree that they become members of the League of Nations with equal representation accorded to all other sovereign and independent Governments.

Mr. BORAH obtained the floor.

Mr. PHELAN. Mr. President——

Mr. BORAH. Does the Senator wish to interrupt me?

The PRESIDENT pro tempore. Does the Senator from Idaho yield to the Senator from California?

Mr. BORAH. I yield for a question.

Mr. PHELAN. The Senator from Tennessee in submitting the amendment just proposed has in view, I believe, the danger of referring to the equality of nations, because it might affect the consideration of our domestic questions by the League of Nations. Am I correct?

Mr. BORAH. I should like, Mr. President——

The PRESIDENT pro tempore. The Senator from Idaho has yielded for a question to be propounded to him and not to the Senator from Tennessee.

Mr. SHIELDS. There will be no discussion on my part.

Mr. BORAH. Very well.

Mr. SHIELDS. I had in mind what is in the covenant and the treaty and the underlying principle and spirit that pervade them.

Mr. PHELAN. Then I understand the Senator is not in any way trying to——

The PRESIDENT pro tempore. Does the Senator from Idaho yield to the Senator from California for a statement or for a question?

Mr. BORAH. I will yield for a statement in reply to the Senator from Tennessee, and then I hope I may be able to proceed.

Mr. PHELAN. I think it is very important to know exactly what the Senator means. I assume, with his consent, that he changed the phraseology by inserting "Governments" for "nations," in order not to embarrass the reservation with an acknowledgment of "the equality of nations," a principle which was rejected at Paris.

Mr. BORAH. Yes; as all other righteous principles were rejected at Paris.

Mr. President, I rise to say that if the League of Nations had been constructed upon the principles announced by the President before he went to Paris there would be no objection whatever in this Chamber to any one of the propositions now included in this reservation. If you will study the principles announced by the President and which apparently had the support of this country prior to the time they were taken possession of by the diplomats of Europe, you will find that they are in perfect harmony with everything expressed in this reservation. The reason why the Senate can not adopt this proposition is that it is out of touch with the covenant itself; the principle of self-determination and the rights of small nations have been absolutely eliminated from the covenant, and to put them in the covenant is to construct an incongruity. That is the reason why, after having discussed this treaty for 14 months upon the basis upon which the diplomats of Europe built it, we hesitate to come back to the principles upon which the President attempted to build it. How strange, indeed, would any principle of justice, of liberty, of the rights of small nations seem in this gigantic autocracy, built upon sheer power and dependent for its existence upon sheer force. You had just as well look among the handiwork of the Kaisers and Czars for the principles of self-determination as to look for them in this structure, designed and built for the purpose of holding in subjection for all time the countless millions who have now been brought under the rule and sway of four or five great powers.

it is because the covenant is constructed upon the theory 300,000,000 dominant people are to control 900,000,000 sub people; and if it is not maintained upon that theory, it f to the ground.

Mr. KING. Mr. President, will the Senator yield?

Mr. BORAH. I yield.

Mr. KING. Does the Senator think that the statement m by the President before going abroad—which, by the way regard as more or less academic and as a statement of a gen doctrine—committed the nations of the world and those accepted that general academic statement to the policy of mediately liberating colonies, dependencies, and dominions, ting all the bonds that united them to the parent Governme and setting them up as independent nations? Does the Sen think that that statement meant that the United States wa liberate the Hawaiian Islands, Porto Rico, and the Philip Islands, and that Great Britain and all other nations might accept that pronouncement of the President's were af wards to let Ireland go and Egypt go and Korea go and Mor go, and other dependencies and territories, controlled by various nations of the world? I do not understand that broad statement or generalization of the President requ that we or any nation that joined the league or that did join the league should go out in a Don Quixote style for purpose of liberating every nation and every people and gi them a government of their own.

Mr. BORAH. When the President announced his princi to the Congress from time to time there was no more ac eulogist in the Senate Chamber than the Senator from U They were not academic propositions at that time. They h only become academic propositions since they were transfor into this autocracy, dominated by the five great powers of world, over 900,000,000 subject peoples. Then they bec "academic," and this became the "practical" proposition wl is before us.

What is the situation with reference to those principles? President was very careful, when Germany signified her de for peace, to transmit to the allied powers a specific statem that peace could only be had upon the basis of his speech u the 8th of January and the addresses thereafter made u that subject. The whole world was familiar with that sp and those addresses. They had been discussed in every c and in every land. There was no place where language spoken that people had not met together and discussed t new policies. The Allies understood them, and Mr. Ll George and other prominent men of Europe and of England discussed them, and had time and time again accepted ther public speech; and when the President sent that message to Allies, the Allies went carefully over those addresses from 8th of January until the 27th of September, and made but exceptions in regard to them. They did not intimate that were academic and impracticable, or that they would no bound by them. They said, "You eliminate the freedon the seas and give us an opportunity to construe the questio reparation and we will make peace with Germany upon principles announced by the President"—not only in his St January speech, which included the 14 points, but in all speeches which followed, at Mount Vernon and New York to the 27th of September. They accepted them, and the P dent replied upon the basis of their acceptance, and the a stice was had upon the basis announced by the President accepted by the Allies.

What I say is, Mr. President, as was so well said by I Keynes in his book, that not a single one of those princi was written into this covenant. On the other hand, the great powers met there and took not only the subject peo that they already had but they incorporated in their domin and under their control millions who prior to that time not been under their domination. There never sat in the tory of the world such an imperialistic body as that which vened at Versailles. That is a general statement, but u that general statement I submit the facts of history.

I want to read—and I trust I shall not be considered di spectful to the English statesmen when I do so—how one of great powers got through with the President's policy. Th an article in a recent number of the Saturday Evening Pos

I sat in the House of Commons and heard Lloyd-George declare the Paris treaty had increased by 800,000 square miles of territory responsibilities of the British Empire. If one adds to that other c tries and territories which in one way or another have come under British control during and since the war and sums up the total result is amazing.

I shall not in the press of time give the entire list. "It g

The Slight Delay

"What this country really needs is a good five-cent cigar," says Wilson's Vice-President, Marshall.

A cigar, a scapegoat, or an escape?

As Wilson's idealism runs into the sand, the Jazz Age starts from a standstill.

The road back from war, even for a population which has declared itself ready, willing and eager to turn its back on everything it has fought for, is not that easy.

Resentment, hatreds, unrelieved emotional tension, whipped up by the war, don't suddenly evaporate with the cease fire. Violence is a hard habit to break. Now the doughboy must use his Springfield at home—to maintain peace—or disturb it.

> No one knows
> No one cares if I'm weary
> Oh how soon they forgot Château-Thierry.

"The next five years will be a very trying time for the World. Civilization in its present form may be severely strained," predicted Britain's Lloyd George shortly after the Armistice. Trying indeed. Civil War in Germany, Revolution in Hungary, Strife in Poland, Roumania, Jugoslavia, Egypt. An upheaval in Russia that seems to freeze violence into a permanent way of life.

*The Doughboy
at Home*

The Senate Debates

Americans, who have averted their eyes, open them to find the reflection of the international turmoil next door and down the street.

In Boston the police strike against a minimum annual wage of $1,100. The resulting pandemonium wins the officers very little but it gives alum-faced, laconic Governor Calvin Coolidge of Massachusetts an opportunity to make a pronouncement to an indignant nation that the electorate will remember. "There is no right to strike against the public safety by anybody, anywhere, any time."

On Wall Street a bomb during lunch hour kills thirty-

The Wall Street Bomb

eight people, maims hundreds, peppers the offices of J. P. Morgan with shrapnel.

In Chicago, race riots leave 38 dead, over 500 injured. In Centralia, Washington, Armistice Day, 1919 is celebrated by an American Legion raid on the local headquarters of the left wing I.W.W. Four dead, six sentenced to prison. In Gary, Indiana, 279,000 steelworkers leave their jobs to protest a 12-hour day and the 100 per cent rise in the cost of living.

Even the telephone operators, the Boston Symphony, and the girls at the *Follies* go out on strike.

Two million malcontents all told.

And the bombs continue. Bombs sent to J. P. Morgan, John D. Rockefeller, Oliver Wendell Holmes, and Attorney General A. Mitchell Palmer, the Fighting Quaker.

What is a strife-weary, good-time-hungry populace to do? Find the culprits, exterminate them, and then sit back and relax? Civil liberties, truth and justice? So's your old man.

Raids, arrests and riots. America sees red—everywhere. S.O.S. There is a new interpretation for the old distress signal—"Ship or Shoot." Some are shot, and many, 3,000 innocent and guilty alike, are shipped.

"Make America safe for Americans" is the cry and the S.S. *Buford* pulls out of New York harbor with 249 aliens and anarchists aboard—"249 blasphemous creatures who

13

The Strikers

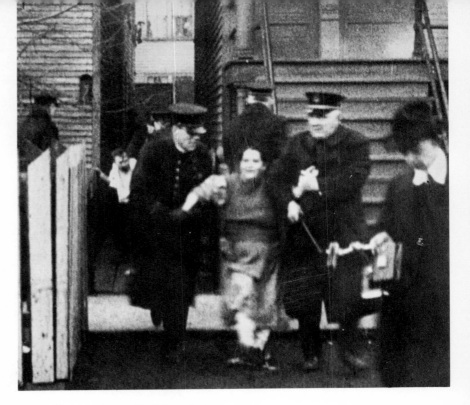

not only rejected American hospitality and assailed her institutions, but also sought by a campaign of assassination and terrorism to ruin her as a nation of free men."

"I believe we should place them all on a ship of stone, with sails of lead, and that their first stopping place should be hell," is one zealot's bon voyage.

Emma Lazarus' "huddled masses" are rejected, her "wretched refuse" is sent back to the teeming shores across seas. The welcome lamp is blown out, the golden door shuts with a bang. Emma Lazarus? Emma Goldman is more

to the point. Emma, editor and anarchist, is the mother of them all—all those terrorists, Communists, Socialists, union organizers. Emma's shipped.

Let Eugene V. Debs run for the Presidency from prison! He disagrees with us. Five Socialist members in the New York Assembly? Kick them out. No matter how much misguided Republicans like Theodore Roosevelt, Jr., and Charles Evans Hughes may object.

Where will it all lead?

"Make America Safe for Americans"

To South Braintree, Massachusetts, where a shoemaker, Nicola Sacco, and a fish peddler, Bartolomeo Vanzetti, are charged with killing a paymaster and his guard and stealing $15,000. The evidence is slim, some say nonexistent, but Judge Webster Thayer declares that they are "anarchist bastards," "dagoes," and "sons of bitches," and that he will "get them good and proper."

It takes seven long years, and the help of such august personages as President Lowell of Harvard, President Stratton of M.I.T., Governor Alvan Fuller of Massachusetts, to do it. It's accomplished over the agonized protests of poets, writers, and politicians around the world.

"Save Sacco and Vanzetti," writes the eminent French author Anatole France. "Save them for your honor, for the honor of your children and of all the generations yet unborn." His plea is seconded by Bernard Shaw, Romain Rolland, Albert Einstein, Henri Barbusse, Walter Lippmann, Fiorello La Guardia, Robert Sherwood, Felix Frankfurter, Heywood Broun, Edna St. Vincent Millay.

"If it had not been for these things, I might have live out my life talking at street corners to scorning men," are Vanzetti's ungrammatical but profoundly moving words to Thayer. "I might have die, unmarked, unknown, a failure. Now we are not a failure. This is our career and our triumph. Never in our full life can we hope to do such work for tolerance, for joostice, for man's understanding of man, as now we do by an accident. Our words—our lives—pains —nothing! The taking of our lives—lives of a good shoemaker and a poor fish peddler—all! That last moment belong to us—that agony is our triumph."

There are riots outside of American embassies in Europe. There are strikes in South America and threats of boycotts on U.S. goods—but the agony takes place with 500 troops guarding the Charlestown, Massachusetts, prison and police boats patrolling the river alongside.

"Long live anarchy," shouts Sacco before he dies.

Anarchy, even as an imaginary threat, has long since died in the mind of most Americans, and Sacco and Vanzetti are sacrificed to a dead fear.

The fear was a long time in dying. Before the country gets over its case of jitters four and a half million supposedly upstanding citizens have become Knights of the Ku Klux Klan—the ultimate perversion of the motto MAKE AMERICA SAFE FOR AMERICANS.

The Klan's purpose is stated succinctly by a member: "A Christian country, free, clean, and democratic: we want

Debs for President?

16

Sacco and Vanzetti

*The Army
Takes Charge*

17

clean politics; we want the elimination of the bootlegger, prostitute, gambler, niggers, Mexicans, Irish, Jews, Germans, Huns, and in fact all foreigners, so they will not be able to appropriate to themselves the policies and destinies of this Great and Glorious American Republic."

The Klan is the legacy of another period of terror—the Reconstruction era in the South. The new Klan is the brainstorm of an impecunious Southern preacher, "Colonel" Simmons, cleverly elaborated by a couple of unscrupulous professional fund raisers named Edward Y. Clark and Elizabeth Tyler.

For an initiation fee of $10, an extra $6.50 for a white robe and hood, and dues of one dollar a month, any "native-born, white, gentile American"—provided he is not a Catholic—can become "a solemn but undignified penguin" and indulge in "bigotry in bedsheets." If his qualities of leadership are conspicuous, there are an infinite number of titles he can aspire to. Nighthawk, Klokann, Klexter, Klagaro, Kladd, Klabee, Kigrapp, Kludd, Klokard, Klaliff, Exalted Cyclops, Kleagle, King Kleagle, Grand Goblin.

Nor do the qualities have to be that conspicuous. When Colonel Simmons outlasts his usefulness, it's a Texas dentist, Hiram Wesley Evans, boasting that he is "the most average man in America," who is elected Imperial Wizard, the Emperor of the Invisible Empire. With the title Hiram miraculously becomes "a wise man, a wonder worker, having power to charm and control."

Morality and patriotism—strong emotions—and in the name of Christianity and the flag, fiery crosses are burned, threats, kidnapings, rapes, mutilations, whippings, tar and featherings, and murders are committed. For the lucky few, the Kleagles, King Kleagles, and Grand Goblins, the monetary returns are in the hundreds of thousands. For the rest, there is the luxury of feeling superior to a lot of your fellow countrymen. That is well worth $16.50.

Will you faithfully strive for the eternal maintenance of white supremacy?

Jesus Christ is the leader of the Ku Klux Klan, and we are for Him. The Jew is not for Him and therefore the Jew has shut himself out of the Klan.

The Pope will sit in the White House when Hell Freezes over.

The slogans and catchwords hide intolerance and crime, intimidation and terror, abracadabra and secret hocus-pocus. Not so secret—the Klan marches in the streets of Tulsa, Oklahoma, in Plainfield, Illinois, down Pennsylvania Avenue in the nation's capital itself.

It is fun to belong, to dress up, to get things done. But what do we belong to? What do the hoods and crosses and robes and double talk signify? What are we really accomplishing? Scandal strips the clan of its pretense of morality. Interior squabbles give citizens who should have known better a chance to think. However, its sinister ground bass continues for a long time thumping behind the strident gaiety of the Jazz Age.

Hiram Wesley Evans,
"The Most Average Man in America"

The Klan Takes Over

Back to Normalcy

"We have worked and suffered for what? For the most colossal farce of all time. . . . The results of the war are nonsense, superb nonsense! Think of Wilson taking on the combined prestige of Lincoln, Cromwell and Christ," says a nation of brand-new cynics and realists. They have found their victims—Wilson, the Reds, any minority—but where is their new Messiah?

Warren Gamaliel Harding, the mahatma of mediocrity, he's our man. BACK TO NORMALCY, is Harding's slogan. There's no such word as normalcy but it garners the Republicans a record majority in the 1920 Presidential election against the Democratic, pro-League candidate, Governor James M. Cox of Ohio.

"*Forward March—straight to the rear!* This is the inaugural command of our new Commander in Chief, President Harding," heckle the liberals. "We are not even to be allowed to stand still, but are to advance backwards just as rapidly as possible—to normalcy by way of stability."

The sneers are drowned out by the cheers for the man who, after the stiff-necked Presbyterian schoolmaster with his nobility and nonsense, is as cozy as slippers, a pipe and that favorite national pastime, the funny papers.

"I am a man of limited talents from a small town. . . . I don't seem to grasp that I am President," says Harding with ingratiating humility after his nomination by "15 men in a smoke-filled room," in Chicago's Blackstone Hotel, and his election by the normalcy-hungry nation. The small town was Marion, Ohio, where Harding, a handsome, affable, lazy boy from the wrong side of the tracks, had married the ambitious daughter of the town big shot and permitted her and a gang of Ohio politicians headed by one Harry M. Daugherty to push him all the way to the White House.

Mrs. Harding has a momentary scruple: "I can see but

one word written above his head if they make him President," she cries in apprehension, "and that word is Tragedy."

But the Ohio Gang sees two words written across their champion's, and patsy's, noble brow—Easy Money. They set up shop in a little green house at 1625 K Street to collect the spoils.

Harding does well by his cronies. Daugherty becomes Attorney-General, Charles Forbes gets the Veterans' Bureau, Albert Fall is made Secretary of the Interior, Thomas W. Miller is Alien Property Custodian, confidence man Gaston Means lands a post high up in the Department of Justice.

There are solid men too—Hoover, Mellon, Hughes, Wallace, Weeks; but they have little or nothing to do with "the poker cabinet" that holds forth on the second floor of the White House. The daughter of a former President, Alice Roosevelt Longworth, takes one quick horrified peak and beats a hasty retreat. "No rumor could have exceeded the reality; the study was filled with cronies. . . . The air heavy with tobacco smoke, trays with bottles containing every imaginable brand of whisky stood about, cards and poker chips ready at hand—a general atmosphere of waistcoat unbuttoned, feet on desk, and spittoons alongside."

For a breath of fresh air, Harding likes "to go out into the country and Bloviate"—bloviate being another word of his own coinage carrying vague hints of blowing off at the mouth, salivating, and oblivion.

His bloviations, according to observer H. L. Mencken, the Thersites of the Jazz Age, were like "a string of wet sponges."

Harding also plays golf, bridge, and bolsters a national fad by taking up "Ping-pong."

Ping-pong and poker notwithstanding, responsibility can be avoided just so long—another lesson that America might have learned early in the decade had it chosen to study Harding's sad case. Unfaced, responsibility pounces, it doesn't slap you on the back. The larger the responsibility,

"Back to Normalcy"

Andrew William Mellon

Teapot Dome—The Investigating Committee

Harry M. Daugherty

Albert B. Fall

the quicker and more terrible the destruction.

Harding, the big handsome hick who campaigned from his own front porch and tried to be everybody's friend, lasted 2 years and 5 months. Like Wilson, the Presidency broke his health and heart. But it wasn't the failure to force his solutions of great problems on an indifferent nation that did it. It was just that the pals he counted on turned out to be anything but good Joes.

Power corrupts, Lord Acton had warned long before.

Harding's power corrupted others than himself: Attorney-General Daugherty indicted for accepting bribes while in office; Forbes imprisoned for doing the Veterans' Bureau out of $200 million in wrongfully condemned merchandise; Miller and Means sent to jail; four suicides in the second ranks; Albert Fall condemned to prison for his part in the Teapot Dome oil scandal, a stench that carried through the whole decade.

Calvin Coolidge: "The Business of America Is Business"

The man who steps in to complete the unfortunate Harding's term of office and stays on for another four years would give no one guilt complexes. If Harding suffered from a boyish urge to be a good fellow liked by everyone, Calvin Coolidge has no such inclination. He isn't even gallant to the ladies.

"Mr. Coolidge, I've made a rather sizable bet with my friends that I can get you to speak three words," says a young woman seated beside him at dinner. "You lose," snaps Coolidge.

"The business of America is business," the new President announces in his flat Vermont accent.

KEEP COOL WITH COOLIDGE, is his campaign slogan when he asks for his temporary lease on the White House to be extended.

KEEP COOL WITH COOLIDGE, is the electorate's reply, and as far as politics, national and international, are concerned, that is just what America does, to the point of total immobility.

"How did you keep yourself fit for the job?" asks Will Rogers.

"By avoiding the big problems," Coolidge replies with nary a twinkle.

When he is confronted with a document on the investment trusts which might have warned against some vague future disaster, he goes down to the White House basement to count a barrel of apples sent by a Vermont admirer instead.

"It is grim, determined, alert inactivity which keeps Mr. Coolidge occupied constantly," writes the author of *A Preface to Morals*, Walter Lippmann. "Nobody has ever worked harder at inactivity, with such force of character, with such unremitting attention to detail . . . the skill with which Mr. Coolidge can apply a wet blanket to an enthusiast is technically marvelous.

"At a time when Puritanism as a way of life is at its lowest ebb among the people, the people are delighted with a Puritan as their national symbol . . . we have attained a

"Keeping cool"

Puritanism de luxe in which it is possible to praise the classic virtues while continuing to enjoy all the modern conveniences. . . . Mr. Coolidge practices a stricter discipline than he preaches and, in a time when politicians are so much more virtuous in talk than they are in their conduct, there is something very engaging about a man who is so much more ascetic in fact than he is in theory."

"I am not going to try and be a great President," Coolidge confides to his friend Dwight Morrow.

"It is as if a hungry man, set before a banquet prepared by master cooks and covering a table an acre in area, should turn his back upon the feast and stay his stomach by catching and eating flies." It is H. L. Mencken heckling again.

Parsimonious, thin-lipped, do-nothing, inert, anesthetic, know-nothing, the Coolidge adjectives hoarded up for future use are not complimentary.

The President takes a nap every afternoon, rocks in his rocker on the White House porch, prowls its corridors in his nightshirt, double checks the household accounts, occasionally tries on an Indian headdress to prove he is a regular fellow—and keeps cool.

34

Two of the hecklers, Will Rogers and H. L. Mencken

Keeping Things Humming

If the nation wants Pennsylvania Avenue to keep cool it is apparently so that Main Street can turn on the heat.

Small-town life is responsible for a lot in our time, good, bad and indifferent, including the new best-selling author, Sinclair Lewis, of Sauk Centre, Minnesota, who acidly observes, "Main Street is the climax of civilization—that this car might stand in front of the Bon Ton Store, Hannibal invaded Rome and Erasmus wrote in Oxford cloisters."

Lewis snipes at the prairie Philistines, but an historic change is underway and Main Street is its subject.

> Dynamo, dynamo
> We're the bunch, We're the bunch
> Dynamo.
> We're alive and coming
> And we'll keep things humming;
> We're surely always on the go.

Sinclair Lewis

35

36

Production at Ford

Another of Lewis's Midwesterners, George Follansbee Babbitt, sings such rousing luncheon-club doggerel (to the tune of "Over There") and he means every word of it.

Babbitt's boosterism stems from no less an authority than Cool Cal himself. Hasn't Cal told the big town Chamber of

Main Street, U.S.A.

Commerce, "Business . . . is the work of the world. It has come to hold a very dominant position in the thoughts of all enlightened peoples. . . . It . . . rests on a higher law. . . . It rests square on the law of service. . . . Government [is

its] vigilant supporter and friend"?

And what about Henry Ford? "There is something sacred about big business," says the Sage of Dearborn. "Anything which is economically right is morally right."

And doesn't Mr. Bruce Barton prove in his dandy book *The Man Nobody Knows* (726,892 copies sold) that Jesus Christ Himself was "the founder of modern business"? That His parables are brilliant examples of the power of advertising? That He had known and followed "every one of the principles of modern salesmanship"? And that He was "the most popular dinner guest in Jerusalem"? The crux of the matter lay in His words, "Wist ye not that I must be about my Father's *business*."

But Mr. Barton isn't going to have it all his way. "The first president of Lions International was Jesus Christ," claims another enthusiast. "I quote you from the Bible. He was 'Lion of the tribe of Judah.' "

The motor of American industry revs up. Mass production means less work and more merchandise, more automobiles, more vacuum cleaners, more tractors, more steel, glass, and rubber to make them, more gasoline and electricity to run them. A huge sign blinks over Manhattan: YOU SHOULD HAVE $10,000 AT THE AGE OF 30, $25,000 AT THE AGE OF 40, $50,000 AT 50." A billion lines of advertising say BUY. A million salesmen, dapper, mobile, fast-talking, say "*Buy*."

How? It is simple. Banker and philanthropist Otto Kahn explains, "The difference between what is available to the rich and to people of small means is diminishing. Installment buying has contributed materially toward this eminently desirable consummation." Main Street is not only urged to buy goods, but to join in an even headier sport, buying stocks. "If, as is claimed, the big companies are making too much money, would it not be well for millions of persons of scanty means to buy the stock of these corporations and thus spread prosperity among the people?" inquires George Horace Lorimer, the conservative, hyper-respectable editor of the *Saturday Evening Post*.

The more we buy, the richer we will all be. And with Cal, Henry Ford, the *Saturday Evening Post*, and the Lord Himself behind us, how can we go wrong?

The Female Revolution

While George Follansbee and Dads everywhere are on the go making and spending money, Mom and Sis are on the go in their own direction. With the vote in their apron pockets they are looking for new worlds to conquer.

"What has become of the useful maiden aunt?" asks an ad for a woman's magazine. "She isn't darning anybody's stockings, not even her own. She's a draftsman or an author, a photographer or a real estate agent. She's the new phenomenon in everyday life."

To make the change more conspicuous, aunts and nieces head from the polling booth to the barbershop, ignoring the warnings of an alarmed press that "the free and easy atmosphere often prevailing in barbershops is unsuitable to the high standard of American Womanhood." What the American women want is a good short shingle and never mind the atmosphere.

There is one hold-out, Miss Mary Pickford, America's Sweetheart herself. "In the epidemic of haircutting that has swept the country, I am one of the few who have escaped. It has been a hard-fought battle, and the problem has occupied many of my waking and sleeping hours. I say 'sleeping' because it often intrudes itself into my dreams. . . . Sometimes it is a dreadful nightmare, when I feel the cold shears at the back of my neck, and see my curls fall one by one at my feet, useless, lifeless things to be packed away in tissue paper with other outworn treasures."

Hair isn't the only thing that is shorn. Skirts are lopped off and bosoms go into a decline. Stockings are flesh-colored, silk and rolled.

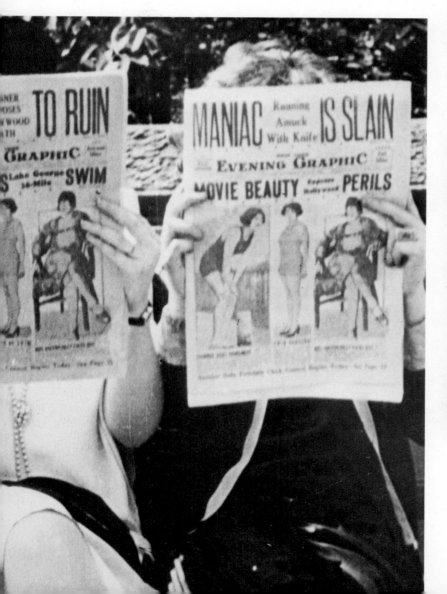

41

"A good short shingle"

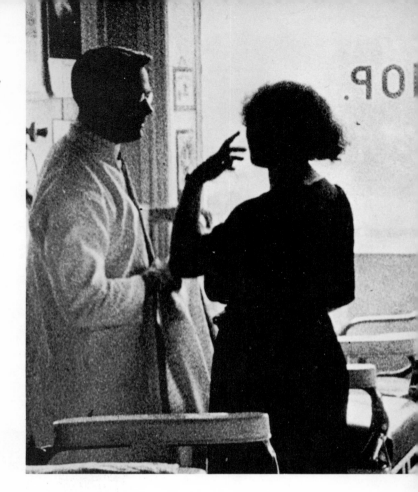

"The low-cut gowns, the rolled hose and short skirts," declaims one university president, "are born of the Devil and his angels, and are carrying the present and future generations to chaos and destruction."

One virtuous and well-meaning group of young ladies chime in their agreement.

> Though standing or sitting, if you please
> With skirts we have well-covered knees.
> Our lines and our curves we don't reveal
> To stranger's stare, but modestly conceal.
> We belong to the crusaders.

Their crusade, alas, is futile. Sumptuary laws aimed at exposed bosoms and short skirts are equally ineffectual in Utah, Virginia and Ohio.

"What if my legs are bad?" writes one poor soul to a fashion expert. "What can I do?"

The finished produ

*America's
Sweetheart*

43

"Walk fast" is the brisk reply. "There are so many legs to look at these days, maybe yours won't be noticed."

Main Street mamas on the go abandon other things besides ankle-length dresses and waist-length tresses. The propriety of bakers' loaves and food in cans has definitely been established. Mom has been freed from the kitchen for a clattering good game of Mah Jong, or a little later, contract bridge. She has time to stand in front of the mirror and say as Eminent Émil, Dr. Coué, recommends: "Day by day in every way I'm getting better and better"; or eventually try her hand at one of those new-fangled crossword puzzles. "Pa, what's a printer's measure in two letters beginning with *E?*"

There are a few reactionaries who regret the decline in quality of the daily bread, the passing of Aunt Sophia's "chow-chow" and apple butter, and Cousin Letta's antimacassars.

Novelist Kathleen Norris is not pleased that the word "obey" is dropped from the marriage ceremony and "debunk" is added to Webster's dictionary.

"No more community living," she says regretfully. "Brothers and sisters, Father and Mother, Grandmother, baby, Aunt Eliza and hired girl—no more interested discussion of family matters, of sewing, cooking, preserving, nursery, books.

"All that is gone. Families get smaller every year, aunts and cousins don't visit as once they did; the one child of the family grows up and goes off to college; Mother goes to Europe, Father to the club."

The machine's to blame, cries another more sensitive writer, Willa Cather. "We have music by machines, we travel by machines—the American people are so submerged in them that sometimes I think they can only be made to laugh and cry by machinery. Nobody stays at home any more; nobody makes anything beautiful any more."

"More women are self-supporting and independent than ever before," H. L. Mencken confirms. "And more

Eminent Emile

women, I suspect, wish they were dead."

But for every spoilsport there are a dozen who speak up for the girls. Dorothy Dix, the eminent seeress whose column of friendly advice has more readers than Mr. Mencken, and the Misses Norris and Cather combined, rushes to the defense.

"The old idea used to be that the way for a woman to help her husband was by being thrifty and industrious, peeling the potatoes a little thinner, and . . . making over her old hats and frocks. . . . But the woman who makes of herself nothing but a domestic drudge . . . is not a help to her husband. She is a hindrance . . . a man's wife is the show window where he exhibits the measure of his achievement. . . . The biggest deals are put across over luncheon tables . . . we meet at dinner the people who can push our

Miss Joan Crawford

Lip painting and rouging

46

fortunes. . . . The woman who cultivates a circle of worthwhile people, who belongs to clubs, who makes herself interesting and agreeable . . . is a help to her husband."

More specifics, Miss Dix. Here they are. "Good looks are a girl's trump card . . . dress well and thereby appear 50 per cent better-looking than you are . . . make yourself charming . . . cultivate bridge and dancing, the ability to play jazz and a few outdoor sports."

For the girl (or matron) on the go, it's Chanel red, and gold lamé (at $22.50 a yard, but it doesn't take that much nowadays)—stripes, going round not up and down (no Gay Nineties figure can survive that treatment)—headbands and pony fur coats—hats like helmets (it takes a shoehorn to get them on your head)—snake shoes and slave bracelets and beads, beads, beads.

Lip painting and rouging can replace the genteel art of water colors in the bright young lady's repertoire of tricks any day. If she sketches anything it will be a new set of eyebrows, not a likeness of her best beau. And if she plays an instrument it won't be "To a Wild Rose" or "The Scarf Dance" on the parlor grand but "Ma—He's Making Eyes at Me" or "Ain't We Got Fun?" on the gramophone.

Her major accomplishment is the Charleston, Charleston.

> Lord how you can shuffle,
> Ev'ry step you do, leads to something new,
> Man I'm telling you, it's a tapazoo.

Loose elbows, loose knees, feet flying, beads flying, slave bracelets ajangle. It doesn't make much sense, but brother, it's fun.

And speaking of brother, what is brother up to? While sister is making her rapid conversion from Gibson Girl to "It" girl, developing the old "S.A." and flapping her galoshes like crazy, brother wraps himself up in his 30-skin raccoon coat, deposits a flask in the hip pocket of his bell-bottom trousers, clamps a battered felt hat on his head and streaks for the local seat of learning.

Charleston,
Charleston!

49

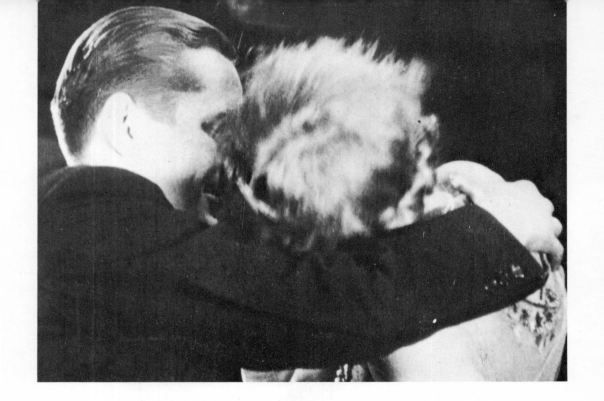

*Joe College
and Betty Coed*

"Going to college, especially in the more backward parts of the country, has come to be a sort of social necessity. It almost ranks with having a bathroom and keeping a car. Thus hordes of the unteachable swarm in, and the poor pedagogues can only gasp in dismay."

Main Street Sheiks and Shebas become Joe College and Betty Coed. "All gods are dead, all wars fought, all faith in man shaken," says Amory Blaine, F. Scott Fitzgerald's undergraduate hero in *This Side of Paradise*.

With brother boozing at the frat and Sis petting in the rumble seat of a Marmon roadster, the front porch and parlor disappear from the family homestead.

The smart new "subdivision" special has a handkerchief lawn (who needs Mum's flower garden, there are long-stemmed American Beauties and hothouse Gardenias at the corner florist). It is "Tudor-bethan" outside. And inside there is a Venetian living room, Spanish Renaissance dining room, Chinese breakfast room, Colonial bedroom and Roman bath.

Even with brother and sis away at State U., these rooms witness some pretty spectacular goings on.

As the Jazz Age continues, according to Fitzgerald, the man who practically invented it: "It became less and less an affair of youth. The sequel was like a children's party taken over by the elders. . . . By 1923 their elders, tired of watching the carnival with ill-concealed envy, had discovered that young liquor will take the place of young blood, and with a whoop the orgy began. . . . A whole race going hedonistic, deciding on pleasure . . . the whole upper tenth of a nation living with the insouciance of grand ducs and the casualness of chorus girls."

Poetess Edna St. Vincent Millay furnishes another credo for the age:

> My candle burns at both ends;
> It will not last the night;
> But ah, my foes, and oh, my friend,
> It gives a lovely light.

Edna St. Vincent Millay

The shellshock of war and the cynicism that Wilson's failure and the whited sepulchers of the Harding administration instill turn into just one more reason for the big party.

Restraint? Bushwah.

Manners? Nertz.

Morals? Banana Oil.

"Sing hallelujah, hallelujah and you'll shoo your blues away."

Let Yourself Go

For the 90 per cent that can't carry on like Fitzgerald's grand ducs and chorus girls there is still more money and more leisure to spend it in than ever before. And you can't neck, pet, cuddle coo, and get blotto all the time.

"Go to a motion picture . . . and let yourself go," the ads urge, and America responds with 40 million paid admissions per week. "Before you know it you are *living* the story—laughing, loving, hating, struggling, winning! All the adventure, all the romance, all the excitement you lack in your daily life are in—Pictures. They take you completely out of yourself into a wonderful new world. . . . Out of the cage of everyday existence! If only for an afternoon or an evening—escape!"

And what will you see when you get there? "Brilliant men, beautiful jazz babies, champagne baths, midnight revels, neckers, petters, white kisses, red kisses, pleasure-mad daughters, sensation-craving mothers . . . the Truth —bold, naked, sensational."

Alice White and Thomas Meighan, Norma and Constance Talmadge, Vilma Banky, Milton Sills, Pola Negri, Rod La Rocque, Gloria Swanson, Anna Q. (for Querentia) Nilsson, the Baby Viking; Garbo and Gilbert— *Flesh and the Devil*; the Great Lover himself—Rodolpho Alfonzo Raffaele Pierre Filibert di Valentina d'Anton-

orty million paid admissions per week"

Alice White

Garbo and Gilbert

58

Gloria Swanson

The "It" Girl

Elinor Glyn and "It"

guolla, ex busboy and gigolo—everybody's sheik. And everybody's Sheba—Betty Blythe. The "It" girl, Clara Bow.

"I wanted to stir up in the cold hearts of the thousands of little fluffy, gold-digging American girls a desire for greater joys in life than are to be found in candy boxes and car rides and fur coats," confesses novelist Elinor Glyn, the red-haired, green-eyed mother of *It*, "a desire to be loved as European women are loved; and as a result, a desire to give as well as to receive."

Mrs. Glyn's desires are realized in spades in the opulent movies of Mr. Cecil B. De Mille, non-Biblical and Biblical, from *Forbidden Fruit, Male and Female*, and *The Golden Bed*, to *The Ten Commandments* and *The King of Kings*.

DeMille with Eddie Rickenbacker and John M. Larson

Pickford and
Fairbanks with
Sid Grauman

62

63

Chaplin and Coogan in "The Kid"

Bathrooms, boudoirs and the Good Book will never be the same. "I have only put bathrooms in three pictures out of the fifty-six I have made," De Mille says midway in his career. "But I will admit they were good ones. Before I started—bathrooms were catch-alls for everything in the family. Now look at them."

If bathrooms and the truth in all its boldness and nudity abash you, there is the soothing sentiment of Lillian Gish and Richard Barthelmess in *Way Down East*, Mary Pickford in *Little Lord Fauntleroy* (curls intact). The high romance of Douglas Fairbanks in *The Thief of Bagdad* and *The Mark of Zorro*. The wistful humor of Chaplin and Jackie Coogan in *The Kid*. The slapstick of Buster Keaton, Harold Lloyd, Fatty Arbuckle. Lon Chaney "the man with a million faces"—every one a hair-raiser. You can even live the story along with Strongheart and Rin-Tin-Tin.

To house all this adventure, romance, excitement, and self-identification, an equally fantastic world of architecture evolves. Chinese, Egyptian, Aztec, Roman, Greek, Byzantine, Balinese. Take your pick. At the Paramount in New York City—the St. Peter's of them all—no choice is necessary. Antiquity and the Renaissance, the Occident and the Orient, are all there under one roof.

There is an Elizabethan Room, a Marie Antoinette Room, an Empire and Colonial Room, a Chinoiserie for ladies who wish a surreptitious cigarette, a music room complete with chamber orchestra if the picture proves too exciting. The lobby, Grand Hall and Hall of Nations rival the baths of Roman emperors, and the auditorium, when you finally reach it, beggars the imagination of Louis XIV himself. There are no indoor fountains at Versailles, at least not ones that change color on cue.

Illusion fosters illusion and the story behind the glamorous silver screen is as bold, naked, sensational, as the movies themselves, and as avidly followed. For tragedy and horror what could rival the early deaths from drink, dope, and dissipation of handsome Wallace Reid, glamorous Alma

Fatty Arbuckle in action

Valentino's funeral

65

Rubens and Barbara LaMarr; the indictment of Roscoe "Fatty" Arbuckle for the unsavory death of a show girl; the unsolved shooting of William Desmond Taylor, with the winsome beauties Mary Miles Minter and Mabel Normand mourning the demise of their love and their careers at one and the same time; the suicide of Olive Thomas, "the most beautiful girl in the world." And finally the untimely passing and fabulous funeral of Valentino himself. Thirty thousand mourners, mounted police charging to drive them back, black-shirted guards protecting the flower-laden coffin.

And the ones who survive scandal and bullets—how they live! They take up where De Mille leaves off. Harold Lloyd's gardens and fountains tumble down the Hollywood hillside in a profusion that rivals Tivoli. The ceiling in Marion Davies' living room is genuine 14-carat gold. Lilyan Tashman's all-white salon features Hollywood's first white piano tied up in an enormous pale blue satin ribbon, and the walls in ill-fated Valentino's Falcon's Lair are prophetically all black.

There is a waiting list among European nobility to visit the magnificent Fairbanks-Pickford seat "Pickfair," and Gloria Swanson takes her baths in a black marble bathroom with a solid gold tub. Tom Mix has his initials up in lights not only on theater marquees but over his Beverly Hills mansion, lest his fans lose sight of him on his hilltop.

No one is going to lose sight of Hollywood, not if Louella Parsons, the Sunday supplements, and dozens of movie magazines can help it.

The movies have one big competitor for America's growing leisure. "Some sunny Sunday very soon," says one of its promoters, "just drive an Overland up to your door —tell the family to hurry the packing and get aboard— and be off with smiles down the nearest road—free, loose and happy—bound for green wonderlands"—or the slough of despond.

And if you are hell-bent anyway, the family Hupmobile makes a perfect portable saloon, or a four-wheeled sofa for youth to flame on.

Automobilitis

*Sinclair Lewis,
wife, and
Model T*

68   *"It's a great car, Henry," says Thomas Edison*

1920 Cadillac

69

Automobilitis replaces spring sickness as America's most fashionable warm-weather disease. Ministers inveigh against it: "If you want to use your car on Sunday, take it out Sunday morning and bring some shut-ins to church and Sunday school; then in the afternoon, if you choose, go out and worship God in the beauty of nature." But church attendance drops.

"In the city of Zenith, in the barbarous twentieth century," according to Sinclair Lewis, "a family's motor indicated its social rank as precisely as the grades of the peerage determined the rank of an English family.... The details of precedence were never officially determined. There was no court to decide whether the second son of a Pierce Arrow limousine should go in to dinner before the first son of a Buick roadster, but of their respective social importance there was no doubt; and where Babbitt as a boy had aspired

1924 Dodge

A 1926 Chrysler car

to the Presidency, his son Ted aspired to a Packard twin
six and an established position in the motored gentry."

Each car had its coat of arms and lofty motto. THOR-
OUGHBRED IS THIS PIERCE ARROW. . . . STUTZ PRESTIGE
RESTS SECURELY UPON STUTZ PERFORMANCE—IT KNOWS
NO MASTER ON THE ROAD. . . . IT PAYS TO OWN A HUPMO-
BILE. . . . WHEN BETTER AUTOMOBILES ARE BUILT BUICK
WILL BUILD THEM. The Packard: ASK THE MAN WHO OWNS
ONE. The Paige: THE MOST BEAUTIFUL CAR IN AMERICA.
. . . THE COUNTRY'S BEST CITIZENSHIP PROCLAIMS THE
CADILLAC THE CAR OF CARS. "Next to my favorite saddle
horse give me this spirited Willys-Knight Six," says Mary
Roberts Rinehart, America's best-loved authoress. The
Nash's "interior is luxuriously appointed with silver-
finished hardware in chaste old Empire mode, silver vanity
case and smoking set, and genuine mohair velvet uphol-
stery." As for the Jordan Play Boy: "Well, I don't expect

to live more than one thousand years," says a bright young thing. "I'll take an enclosed car for my wheel chair days. Right now give me a Playboy and make it carmine, a friendly pilot in a coonskin coat—a road that never ends—and I don't care where we go."

All the loose talk and luxury appointments rattle the Tin Lizzy into oblivion as Henry Ford spends two million dollars to advertise her successor and to stir up public curiosity to a frenzied peak. One million New Yorkers mob the showrooms the first day. Mounted police are called to

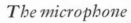

The microphone

keep back the crowds in Cleveland. A pedestal for the shiny new Model A is built in Kansas City so that all may see.

"Everybody is rushing to go somewhere where they have no business, so they can hurry back to the place where they should never have left," is Will Rogers' comment, as brisk as an October ride in a Bear Cat rumble seat.

Although movies and motor cars have a head start, before the decade is far advanced a new gadget is taking its tithe out of the nation's leisure. Radio, begun in a tent on a roof in Pittsburgh, is soon blanketing the nation. Families crowd round while Dad clamps the crystal set to the telephone, lowers the cat's whisker and, Hark!—It is Harry Horlick and the A and P Gypsies plinking "Two Guitars," Harry Reser and the Clicquot Club Eskimos bubbling away like their sponsor's ginger ale. For a growing horde of radio listeners Walter Damrosch benignly leads the way through Tchaikovsky and Rimsky Korsakov, Jessica Dragonette warbles the Italian Street Song for Coca-Cola. There are Miss Olive Palmer, the Palmolive girl; the Dun-

The Clicquot Club Eskimos

An early radio set

Jessica Dragonette

Billy Jones and Ernie Hare,
"The Happiness Boys"

74

can Sisters; Will Rogers imitating President Coolidge, and President Coolidge imitating himself.

"It is inconceivable," says Secretary of Commerce Herbert Hoover, "that we should allow so great a possibility for service, for news, for entertainment, for education and for vital commercial purposes to be drowned in advertising chatter," not long after the first commercial (ten uninterrupted minutes recommending a Long Island real estate development) goes on the air.

As the radio set evolves from the earphone stage to the multi-tubed, many-knobbed, hand-carved Venetian, Colonial, Jacobean, and Japanned monstrosities that dominate the nation's living rooms, advertising grows apace. But it is a new kind of music that makes the biggest dent in the nation's eardrums.

"All over the country," complains Charles Merz in *The Great American Bandwagon*, "the trombones blare and the banjos whang and the clarinets pipe the rhythm. All over the country the same new tunes that will be generations old before the week is out are hammered home at the same vast audience from a hundred different places. Oom-pah-pah, oom-pah-paah. I got the blue-hoo-hoos, I got the blue-hoo-hoos . . ."

Anyone who has ignored the jazz of the Jazz Age before can do so no longer. To the nation's million gramophones another, even more pervasive, voice is joined.

The art form that gave the era its name has already been reviled. "Its influence is as harmful and degrading to civilized races as it always has been among the savages from whom we borrowed it," says a spokesman for education. "If we permit our boys and girls to be exposed indefinitely to this pernicious influence, the harm that will result may tear to pieces our whole social fabric."

A doctor discovers it is a substitute for bootleg hooch. "Reason and reflection are lost and the actions of the person are directed by the stronger animal passions. In other words, jazz affects the brain through the sense of hearing, giving the same results as whisky or any other

Vaughn de Leath

Ed Wynn

Sound effects

Fred Allen

Paul Whiteman

alcoholic drinks taken into the system by way of the stomach."

The jazz that paddled upstream from the bordellos of New Orleans and was dished out along with the local rot gut at the gangster-infested honky-tonks of Chicago—the jazz sung by Bessie Smith, and Ma Rainey, played by King Oliver, Kid Ory, Jelly Roll Morton and his Red Hot Peppers, Louis Armstrong and the Hot Five, Bix Beiderbecke and the Wolverines, Fletcher Henderson and Duke Ellington—gets cleaned up by Paul Whiteman, sweetened by Vincent Lopez and Guy Lombardo. It even gets as far as Carnegie Hall, Town Hall and the Metropolitan Opera. But there is still enough of the twang, blare and grit left to betray its origins.

The popular singing voice of the Roaring Twenties comes high and through the nose. It sings the verse all the way through and gives you two versions of the chorus with a bonus of grace notes and vo-de-yo-dos thrown in.

Gene Austin threatens retribution with "Someday Sweetheart" and promises bliss with "My Blue Heaven." Marion Harris serves notice that "There'll Be Some Changes Made"—then explains why "It Had to Be You." You feel an unforgettable zing and elation while Ruth Etting is "Shaking the Blues Away"; an inexpressible melancholy when Helen Morgan sings "Why Was I Born?" or "Can't Help Lovin' That Man." And finally when a youngster named Vallee claims he is just "A Vagabond Lover," and insists upon raising the stein for Dear Old Maine, you accept the fact, although you may not approve the sentiments in a Yale alumnus.

Reedy, nasal or raucous, there is never any question about words or tune in the twenties. And what words and tunes!

Sad songs:

> All alone ev'ry evening
> All alone feeling blue
> Wond'ring where you are, and how you are
> And if you are all alone too.

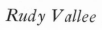
Rudy Vallee

Irving Berlin

79

And lots of glad songs:

> Sleepy time gal
> You're turning night into day
>
> Nothing could be finer
> Than to be in Carolina
> In the morning
>
> Yes, Sir, that's my baby
> No, Sir, I don't mean maybe
> Yes, Sir, that's my baby now.

Whacky songs:

> Yes! we have no bananas
> We have no bananas today

And bad songs:

> Ooooooooooh, do it again
> I may say no no no no no but do it again

To keep up with the demand, Irving Berlin writes one a week. Jerome Kern imbeds a half-dozen unforgettable hits in his trend-setting score for the best-selling novel by Edna Ferber, *Show Boat*. Walter Donaldson, Vincent Youmans, Dick Rodgers and Cole Porter. As the decade progresses a crowd of gifted song writers fall in behind the masters. Operettas dwindle as revues and musical comedies, drawing heavily on jazz motifs, move in.

Lady Be Good stars a brother-and-sister team with a memorable last name—Astaire. *Oh, Kay* introduces a pert British girl called Gertrude Lawrence and a great score: "Someone to Watch Over Me," "Maybe" and "Clap-a Yo Hands." *Funny Face* boasts a tune called "S'Wonderful."

Fred and Adele

Everyone is clapping his hands and exclaiming s'wonderful about George Gershwin. These shows and practically everything else he writes hits the Jazz Age right where it lives.

"He alone, actually expresses us," says a contemporary music critic after hearing his "Rhapsody In Blue," "He is the Present with all its audacity, impertinence, its feverish delight in motion, its lapse into rhythmical exotic melancholy. Mr. Gershwin writes without the smallest hint of self-consciousness and with unabashed delight in the stridency, the gaucheries, the joy and excitement of life as it is lived right here and now. . . . He possesses the genius for molding the crude material of jazz into art forms that are mirrors of the exciting panorama that just now is passing before us."

Sentimental, hard-boiled, jolly, down-in-the-mouth, the Jazz Age is reflected mirror-clear in its music.

George Gershwin

Buy, Buy, Buy

In an era of songs, one song puts it more concisely than
any other.

> Blue skies smiling at me
> Nothing but blue skies do I see.*

And the most important bit of blue sky in the land is the
narrow strip over Wall Street. With Calvin Coolidge's
thin-lipped blessing, the lid has been removed. The sound
of the stock-ticker, not Guy Lombardo, is the sweetest
music this side of heaven. Thanks to Mr. Secretary Mellon
and a few other sympathetic types, taxes for tycoons are
slashed, tariffs raised to protect soaring domestic prices
from "unfair" foreign competition. With all that spare
cash floating about, the stock market takes on a new signifi-
cance. Shares rise—30 points in three years. The turnover
doubles—a pale shadow of things to come. Mysticism has
invaded the workaday world of making and spending
money. The priests of this new religion are the captains of

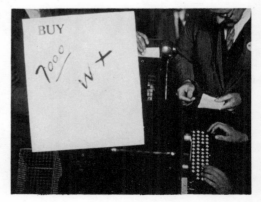

* Copyright 1927 Irving Berlin. Copyright Renewed. Reprinted by Permission of Irving Berlin Music Corporation.

The Exchange

On the floor

Up, up—and up

86

industry and finance themselves, William C. Durant and John J. Raskob of General Motors, Charles E. Mitchell of the National City Bank and a whole corps of profits prophets.

There is of course the small matter of the farmers. With more produce thanks to tractors and fewer buyers thanks to tariffs, with prices dropping and mortgages rising, no one dreams of the tillers of the soil in the new get-rich-quick philosophy. "No complicated scheme of relief, no plan for government-fixing of prices, no resort to the public Treasury, will be of any value. Simple and direct methods put into operation by the farmer himself are the only real sources of restoration," says the New England farm boy, Calvin Coolidge, loftily.

And there is the rather large unpleasantness in Florida. Not too many moons ago the ads read: "Will you take the priceless gift of—LIFE! Bronzed, erect old men. Women delighting in new cream-and-rose complexions. Round and bronze children. Handsome full-figured youngsters. These are evidences of the extraordinary vitality and superb health that come from living under the tropical skies of Coral Gables. And when you see these people you will believe, as we do, that the only American tropics will add years to your life and will add new pleasures and delights to each year.". . . "Sparkling sapphire waters caressing glistening white sands.". . . "Countless birds singing rare melodies in the emerald foliage."

William Jennings Bryan rushes down to add his enthusiasm in pear-shaped tones from an awninged barge on a Coral Gable lagoon. Gilda Gray employs her famous shimmy to entice settlers to this new heaven on earth.

There are skeptics. One is novelist Theodore Dreiser, who reports back, "What a bluff! What a gouge!" The state, Dreiser discovers, is covered with mangy pines rather than palms. It rains frequently. Frost falls in the "frost-proof" cities. The roads are bad and the birds do not sing. "Above all it is meretricious and worse, vulgar . . . luxury to the point of nausea." But Dreiser is a famous atheist. He

On the beach

Gilda Gray
leads the way

Miami Beach

On the beach

wouldn't know heaven if he saw it.

However, another skeptic is God Himself, Who flattens the teetering papier-mâché Florida pyramid with one spectacular hurricane. Lagoons once more become swamps, sprawling subdivisions whose lots have been sold a dozen times over at increasingly exorbitant prices are suddenly revealed as the uninhabitable wildernesses they always were. A horde of prospective bronze homesteaders and peaches-and-cream opportunists return north sadder, wiser and poorer than when they departed.

But why be morbid? The exceptions merely prove the rule that now we are dealing with the very tickets to prosperity and heaven on earth themselves—common stock in AT and T, General Electric, Montgomery Ward, Radio. Don't be a knocker.

On the beach

"People wire in 'Buy me some stocks.'" Will Rogers is on hand to describe the situation as usual. "The brokers answer, 'What kind?' And the buyers wire back, 'Any kind; the Republicans are in, ain't they all supposed to go up?'" And they do go up. Five points, ten points, twenty points.

Never saw the sun shining so bright
Never saw things going so right.

Clear Thinking
and Clean Living

"This law will be obeyed in cities large and small, and in villages, and where it is not obeyed it will be enforced. The law says that liquor to be used as a beverage must not be manufactured. We shall see that it is not manufactured. Nor sold, nor given away, nor hauled in anything on the surface of the earth or under the earth or in the air."

Wilson is still President when these stalwart, if over-optimistic, words are uttered by a new kind of civil servant, John F. Kramer, Prohibition Commissioner. An exultant Anti-Saloon League had already welcomed in "an era of clear thinking and clean living."

However, before the noble experiment of the 18th Amendment to the Constitution has a chance to succeed, the Spartan idealism that engendered it dies. Denied legal satisfaction the country's thirst becomes monumental.

Who knows who the first bootlegger was? The title of the first speak-easy proprietor is claimed for a boniface in

Manhattan's raffish, unconventional Greenwich Village named Barney Gallant, who buys a Washington Square address, cuts an eye-level slot in the front door and begins a national ritual for parched citizens.

"No, I don't know you," says an invisible mouth below the wary eyes.

"Joe sent me," is the hieratic response.

"Membership card? Money? That's different. Come right on in and name your poison."

The bootlegger replaces the family doctor as the character most frequently called on in distress. The speakeasies house the symposia of the jazz generation.

"This joint is the bee's knees and the cat's pajamas (or meow) all rolled into one," the cry goes out as uptown mansions and dingy farmhouses beside the nation's highways respond to the call "How dry I am!"

Every sip of Scotch, every swallow of gin, is a violation of the law of the land, but happy scofflaws are sipping and chug-a-lugging from coast to coast.

Hip flasks and teacups, the ships can't bring the stuff in fast enough to keep them filled. Alky cooking in hideaway booze factories turns out raw whisky, or worse, on a mass-

"Joe sent me"

"Come right on in and name your poison"

Distribution . . .

. . . and consumption

Izzy and Moe

production basis. Barns, caves, corncribs, rendering works, even old churches, are called into service as stills. But the customer is always told: "It's just off the boat. It's still dripping with salt water."

What matter if 1,565 people die of unwisely quenched thirst in a single year? Who cares if 75,000 caterers to the public's liquid needs are arrested per annum at a cost of $20 million? Didn't a U.S. Representative get caught bringing six trunkloads of the stuff through customs? Didn't Senator Brookhart of Iowa admit that full flasks were *de rigueur* as door prizes at some congressional parties? Didn't the genuine article flow like water at those poker parties that Warren Gamaliel himself used to throw?

White Mule and Jackass Brandy, Panther Whisky, Goat Whisky, White Lightning and Jersey Lightning, Soda Pop Moon, Yack Yack Bourbon, Straitsville Stuff, Jamaica

101

La Guardia and his beer test

Ginger. What matter if you're blinded and paralyzed—the kick's the thing.

The prohibition agent becomes the Till Eulenspiegel of the time. Izzy Einstein and Moe Smith, joint avoirdupois circa 500 pounds, are the heroes of a thousand raids. To vary their routine they pose as football players, violinists, gravediggers. They wear false whiskers, cutaways, mud-stained jerseys, black face, anything to get where they can collect their evidence.

"A few more Izzies scattered over the country and the U.S. would be bone dry, parched and withered," states the Brooklyn *Eagle*.

Thanks to Izzy and Moe there are 4,392 arrests, 5 million bottles of booze worth $15 million go down the drain.

But it is just a drop in the bucket. Things get so bad that Elmer Davis, in 1926, envisions "a future when not one but all of the cafés and speak-easies and blind tigers shall be maintained by federal agents for the sublime purpose of gathering evidence; when each and every one of us, on the government payroll as prohibition investigators, shall buy our drinks from these government agencies on a Treasury expense account and acquire our wealth by shaking down the proprietors; and nobody will care, because it will all come out of tax money."

Mr. Davis isn't being as fantastic as he thinks. "The prohibition service proved to be a training school for boot-leggers," admits one commissioner. "While in the service, they naturally learn all the ropes of the underworld as well as the government's methods in attempting to apprehend and convict violators.... Naturally, when leaving the service of the prohibition forces, they are sought after by those engaged in the illicit business."

The illicit business is big business.

Between hooch and beer the profits of rumrunning and bootlegging run into real dollars, tens of millions. The competition is stiff. Behind the camaraderie of the Greenwich Village basement awash with phony spirits and the country club dance afloat in fusel oil (32,000 speak-easies in New York, 10,000 in Chicago) are the occupational

Occupational hazards

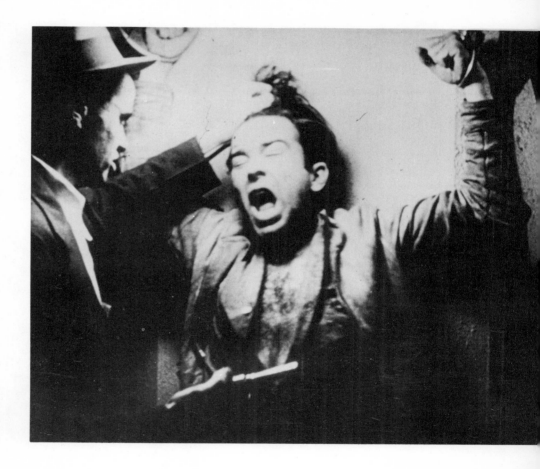

Dion O'Bannion's $10,000 casket

*"Legs" Diamond
and friend*

hazards of a very lucrative industry. Hijacking. And if road blocks and slugs in rear tires don't turn the trick—murder.

As bootlegging becomes more competitive, gangsters take their strong arms and small arms into greener fields. Laundries, garages, florists, bakeries. Why shouldn't they pay a reasonable fee for useful advice and protection? Preventing bombs from arriving through your front window, or keeping acid out of the sheets, is certainly worth a modest monthly fee; and safety is insured since protector and predator are one and the same. If you resist the highly persuasive sales spiel, or object that the situation seems a little artificial, then a representative from Consolidated Rackets, Inc., will convince you with a routine business call.

The satraps of this world beneath the world have colorful names—Jack "Legs" Diamond, Dion O'Bannion, Johnny Torrio, Klondike O'Donnell, the terrible Gennas, and Machinegun Kelly—and their favorite playground is that "toddlin' town," Chicago. Cowboys and Indians have become old hat. Now it's cops and robbers, with more often than not the robbers coming out on top. If now and then there is a pinch for appearance's sake, the legal department of Rackets Unlimited are specialists in "putting in the fix" and "beating the rap."

Occasionally a law enforcement officer goes against established custom. One memorable evening, Detective Broderick of New York lifted trigger-happy Legs Diamond from a Broadway theater seat, carried him into the street and dumped him head foremost into the nearest trash can with a firm recommendation that he stay there or get out of town.

But regulation more often than not is an inside job without regard for due process of law—seven men lined up against the wall of a Chicago garage on St. Valentine's Day and mowed down by some gentlemen who arrive and depart in a big black limousine and borrowed policemen's togs.

Horatio Alger no longer has a corner on stories of suc-

cess. Henry Ford, Thomas Edison and Andrew Carnegie move over for public enemy number one, Alphonse "Scarface" Capone, who rises from a small-time hoodlum to control a cartel of crime and vice that grosses a hundred million dollars a year.

With an army of 700 thugs and gunmen, Little Caesar can do pretty much what he wants in a city of three million . . . and take his winters in a 25-room Florida mansion to boot.

"I don't want to break the hearts of people who love me," says Scarface Al about his hoodlum playmates. "Maybe I can make them think of their mothers and sisters and if they think of them they'll put away their guns and treat their business like anyone else. After working hours they'll go home where they belong."

The fellow sounds reasonable enough if you discount those 500 brutal gangland slayings that litter Chicago sidewalks while Capone rules the roost.

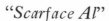

"Scarface Al"

St. Valentine's Day, Chicago, 1929

RECTOR AND WOMAN CHOIR SINGER FOUND MURDERED IN FIELD

New Brunswick, N. J., Clergyman and His Gardener's Wife Disappeared on Thursday.

BOTH SHOT THROUGH HEAD

Authorities Say Nature of the Wounds Precludes Theory a Suicide Compact.

HAD LONG BEEN FRIENDLY

Dr. Edward W. Hall Had Been Rector of Church of St. John the Evangelist for Ten Years.

The bodies of the Rev. Edward [...] Hall, rector of the Protestant Episco[pal] Church of St. John the Evangelist [...] New Brunswick, N. J., and of M[iss] Eleanor Mills, a member of the chu[rch] choir and wife of the church garde[ner] were found lying side by side under [a] tree in a field across the Raritan R[iver] from New Brunswick yesterday mo[rn]ing.

There were two bullet wounds in [the] back of the man's head and one in [the] woman's forehead. The location [and] course of the bullets showed plai[nly] that it was a case of double mur[der] rather than a suicide compact but [the] identity of the murderer and motive [re]mained a mystery last night.

The investigating authorities leane[d to] the jealousy theory. Scattered about [the] bodies was a litter of papers, in wh[ich] were found three notes in a woman['s] handwriting which indicated that [the] choir singer was in love with the cler[gy]man.

There remained the possibility [that] robbery was the motive. Dr. Hall, [who] was wealthy, had the reputation [of] carrying a large amount of money w[ith] him at all times, and his money [and] his watch were missing when the bo[dies] were discovered.

It was pointed out, however, that [the] money and watch might have b[een] taken to conceal the real motive. A [new] mystery was disclosed early this m[orn]ing when the authorities said that [wit]nesses had seen a woman enter the [front] door of the Hall home in New Br[uns]wick at 3 o'clock last Friday morn[ing,] a few hours after Dr. Hall and Miss Mills are believed to have been killed. These witnesses are William Phillips, night watchman at the New Jersey State Women's College, across from the Hall home, and Allan Bennett, who lives next to the Halls. Attracted by the barking of dogs, the men investigated and saw a woman of medium height, dressed in a polo coat, cross the lawn of the Hall grounds and enter the house.

Had Been Missing Since Thursday.

Dr. Hall and Mrs. Mills had been missing since Thursday evening, and the condition of the bodies when they were

Can't Tax Liquor if Holder Neither Made Nor Sold It

CINCINNATI, Ohio, Sept. 16.—A ruling that the Internal Revenue Department cannot legally collect taxes for the possession of liquor if the possessor had neither manufactured nor sold it, was passed by Federal District Judge J. W. Peck today.

The ruling was made on the demurrer of a man who had been previously convicted of illegal possession of liquor and against whom the Government attempted to foreclose a tax lien of $2,000.

The ruling means the loss of thousands of dollars yearly to the Revenue Department, Government officials say. No redress can be had by persons who have paid such taxes in the past, however, in the opinion of Federal officials here.

N. Y. C. BREAKS OFF STRIKE CONFERENCE

Officials Announce No Further Parleys With Shopmen

[...] ferences between representatives of the shop craft employes on strike and officers of the New York Central Lines terminated this evening without an agreement being reached.

"The New York Central Lines were ready and willing throughout successive conference to abide by and fulfill to the letter and spirit the memorandum of agreement reached at Baltimore. The representatives of the shop crafts, however, attempted to interject questions not mentioned in the text and clearly outside of the agreement, insisting that these matters be included. To this the railroad management could not agree."

BRITAIN PREPARES TO [...] CALLS ON DOMINIONS [...] SMYRNA WIPED OUT [...]

ONLY RUINS LEFT IN SMYRNA

Fire Has Swept the City Proper and Is Raging in Suburbs.

AMERICANS GIVE SOLE AID

Naval and Relief Forces Grapple With Task of Succoring 200,000 Christians.

British Land Large Forces A[...] They Begin Entrenching

CONSTANTINOPLE, Sept. 16 (Ass[ociated Press]).—[Turk]ish forces, with heavy artillery, have be[en placed] in the Dardanelles, prepared for any event.

The British forces which landed are [...] Further contingents are on the way.

Confidence that they can check an[y attack on] the historic waterway was expressed b[y] General Shuttleworth, who is in com[mand of] French and Italian battalions.

The British officials are confident [...] have not yet held Constantinople as [...] It is officially announced that Field [Marshal] is expected to arrive here soon.

Sir Harry Lamb, British High Com[missioner is con]ferring with Mustapha Kemal Pasha, [...] The conference was over the political, [...]

[...] throes of terror.

Rescue work among the ruins is proceeding slowly, the Kemalists leaving the fire victims to their fate.

The catastrophe is so vast that only the collective efforts of the allied nations can cope with it.

Swim Out to Our Warships.

When the fire was at its worst the American destroyers Lawrence and Litchfield were almost swamped by thousands of maddened survivors who plunged into the water in the darkness of night and swam out to the vessels, imploring piteously to be saved. The American bluejackets rescued hundreds

PUTS RESOLUTION IN HOUSE

It Calls on President to Aid in Re-establishing Political and Industrial Peace.

Special to The New York Times.

WASHINGTON, Sept. 16.—Represent[ative]

The professionals by no means have a corner on crime. Amateurs are busy too. If the public gets bored with mayhem as a hardheaded business proposition, it can amuse itself with the exploits of those unfortunates who resort to it as an avocation.

When an Episcopal minister, Edward Wheeler Hall, and his choir soloist Mrs. Eleanor Mills were found murdered under a New Jersey crabapple tree in 1922, the press was apparently too occupied by lurid happenings in Hollywood to pay much heed. However, when the widow, Mrs. Hall, her two brothers Willie and Henry Stevens, and her stockbroker cousin Henry de la Bruyère Carpender are indicted for murder four years later, the press and an obedient nation hop to attention. Propriety masking passion, religion dancing attendance on illicit romance, these heady combinations bring 300 reporters to the scene of the trial.

Mary Roberts Rinehart, Revivalist Billy Sunday, Playgirl Peggy Hopkins Joyce, Damon Runyon, the victim's husband James Mills and his flapper daughter Charlotte, are drafted into service to file copy. The New York *Mirror*, the paper responsible for breaking the case, rents a New Brunswick house and hires a butler to make its staff comfortable. A daily average of 500,000 words of lurid prose go out over 60 special lines to an eager world. Readers aren't disappointed. Love letters from "babykins" to "Gypsy Queen" are turned over to the press by Mills. "Swarms of comic witnesses, who claim to have been standing about, 7 tiers deep, made such affairs as the death of Julius Caesar look by comparison like dark and impenetrable mysteries," observes crime analyst Edmund Pearson.

Star of the grim travesty is Jane Gibson, a local character who rides a mule, raises pigs and claims to have witnessed it all. Mortally ill of cancer, she is brought to court on a stretcher with doctor and nurse in attendance. "I've told the truth, so help me God. And you know it," "The Pig Woman" denounces "Iron Widow" Hall who in 18 days of testimony has never flinched. After 5 hours' de-

"The Pig Woman"

Willie Stevens, Mrs. Hall, Henry Stevens, and Cousin Henry Carpender

liberation the jury brings in a verdict of "not guilty."

The crime is never solved, and the public and press move on to what Damon Runyon calls "The Dumbbell Murder," an even more squalid affair involving a blond Long Island housewife, Ruth Snyder, her corset salesman lover Judd Gray and the unfortunate Mr. Snyder, whom they kill with a sash weight, some picture wire and a bit of chloroform. Although, thanks to a willingness on both defendants' parts to confess the crime for his partner, the verdict seems a foregone conclusion, the list of attendants at the courthouse is filled with the famous and the notorious. In the front row again are Mary Roberts Rinehart, Billy Sunday and Peggy Hopkins Joyce, joined by Will *The Story of Philosophy*" Durant, theatrical impresario David Belasco, director D. W. Griffith, Aimee Semple McPherson, and Damon Runyon, who remarks with undisguised distaste that Mrs. Snyder is "chilly-looking as an ice-cream cone" and Gray resembles "a slowly collapsing lump of tallow."

The press, not satisfied with recording the verdict of "guilty," pursues the malefactors to the death house where a photographer from the New York *Daily News* straps a camera to his ankle and snaps a forbidden picture of the unfortunate blonde at the moment of her electrocution, an

Ruth Snyder

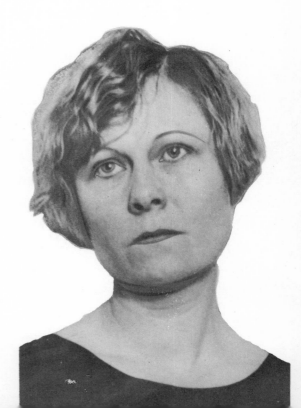

THE MOST TALKED OF PICTURE EVER PUBLISHED.—Due to the tremendous interest in the execution of Mrs. Ruth Snyder and widespread discussion of the whole question of capital punishment, THE NEWS today republishes what is perhaps the most remarkable unofficial and exclusive death room picture ever taken and one which may be the last of an execution of a woman in America. It shows Mrs. Snyder strapped into the Sing Sing chair, helmeted, an electrode strapped to bared right leg as lethal current surged through her.

act which marks the low point of journalism for a decade as undisciplined in its reportage as it is on the dance floor.

City editors greedy for circulation may label the Hall-Mills and Snyder-Gray cases "the crime of the century" in rapid succession, but "the crime of the decade" is without question the cold-blooded murder of a fourteen-year-old Chicago youth named Bobby Franks by a pair of rich teen-agers with astronomic I.Q.'s—Richard Loeb and Nathan Leopold.

College graduates at eighteen and nineteen, pursuing advanced courses at the University of Chicago, the two youths make an unholy alliance to commit the perfect crime. Clarence Darrow, the champion of the underdog, agrees to take the defense.

If America wishes an object lesson in the ultimate destination of a precocious thrill-for-thrill's-sake philosophy, it can find it in the thirty days of testimony concerning these "irresponsible, weak, diseased" youths. It can also treat itself to an extension course in Freudian psychology, a mythology for moderns which has been tapping away at the public subconscious and will be used throughout the

Leopold and Loeb

decade as just one more excuse for misbehaving. Id, super ego, complexes, repressions, inhibitions, we've all got them and the grownups are to blame. "We studied Freud, argued Jung, checked our dreams by Havelock Ellis and toyed lightly with Adler," writes thirteen-year-old Elizabeth Benson in an article "The Truth about the Younger Generation" in *Vanity Fair*. "To hell with Sigmund," says her irreverent elder, Ben Hecht. "He's corrupted immorality."

Thanks to Freud and Darrow, Leopold and Loeb get life and 99 years instead of the electric chair, and America continues to rationalize its guilt away.

Mr. Darrow, with his unerring instinct for a nation's inconsistencies, heads for the headlines once more. This time it takes him to the hot, dusty valley town of Dayton, Tennessee, where a young fellow named Scopes is charged with teaching his high school students the heretical tenets of Darwin.

Up for trial is not Scopes so much as fundamentalist old-time religion and to its defense rushes the silver-tongued Orator of the Platte, William Jennings Bryan.

Corn liquor and Coca-Cola, hymnbooks and slogans cribbed from the Apocalypse—half carnival, half revival meeting, the trial reaches its climax on the fourteenth day, when the court adjourns to the lawn to accommodate the crowds and the real issues come out into the open as well.

Voices rise. Tempers boil. Darrow shouts his purpose—

Darrow in Tennessee

Darrow and
clients

"The Poor Mountebank"

"To show up fundamentalism, to prevent bigots and ignoramuses from controlling the educational system of the United States." Bryan shouts back he is there "to protect the word of God from the greatest atheist and agnostic in the United States."

Darrow loses the case. Scopes' fine, $100, is paid by the Baltimore *Sun* which has sent professional iconoclast H. L. Mencken to report the proceedings. But Bryan's victory is bitter. He and his doctrine of revealed religion have been held up to merciless ridicule, not only by Darrow, but by Mencken and his journalistic buddies. The real victim, Bryan, dies of apoplexy before he can leave town.

Mencken pursues his victim past the grave. "There stood the man who had been thrice a candidate for the Presidency of the Republic," he writes. "There he stood in the glare of the world, uttering stuff that a boy of eight would laugh at. The artful Darrow led him on: he repeated it, ranted for it, bellowed it in his cracked voice. So he was prepared for the final slaughter. He came into life a hero, a Galahad, in bright and shining armor. He was passing out a poor mountebank."

With Bryan and his ridiculed faith go a few more of the Jazz Age's inhibitions.

The Last Refuge of the Highborn

"Pack up your sins and go to the devil in hades" * goes the popular song, only there doesn't seem to be a devil or a hell to go to any more.

"Only on the firm foundation of unyielding despair can the soul's habitation henceforth be safely built," Bertrand Russell announces at the beginning of the decade.

"I used to believe in Hell and Heaven. Now I don't know what to think, but, anyway, I don't spend any time worrying about it," answers a voice from Main Street.

"Religion Is A Solid Investment" is another popular theory, and the Swedish Immanuel Congregational Church of New York offers to all who contribute the amount of $100 to its building fund "an engraved certificate of investment in preferred capital stock in the Kingdom of God."

Or maybe it's a matter of athletic prowess. Sermons are preached on:

117

* Copyright 1922 Irving Berlin. Copyright Renewed. Reprinted by Permission of Irving Berlin Music Corporation.

Samson—the World's Strong Man
Jacob—the Great Wrestler
Enoch—the Long-Distance Walker
David—the Pinch Hitter
Saul—the Man Who Fumbled the Ball
Jesus—the World Champion

But for every $10 spent on movies, $7 on cosmetics, the Protestant churches get 9¢.

The most conspicuous religious figure of the decade is auburn-haired evangelist Aimee Semple McPherson, who disappears from the limelight one May afternoon into the Pacific Ocean clad in a green bathing suit, reappears 36 days later in the desert near Douglas, Arizona, with nary a drop of water or perspiration on her soignée person, the

Sister Aimee

Billy Sunday

Billy in action

victim, she claims, of kidnapers named "Rose" and "Jake" and "Steve." A crowd of 130,000 cheers her triumphant return to her thriving Angelus Temple but gradually the Sister's tale appears to be full of more holes than holiness. Was that Aimee occupying a love nest in Carmel? Was it she in the blue Chrysler outside of Santa Barbara? Was she just a lovesick matron and not a martyr after all?

"It was a story made for the period," says an old California neighbor, Carey McWilliams; "a period that invested the trivial with a special halo, that magnified the insipid, that pursued cheap sensationalism with avidity and passion. . . . It was a kind of compendium of all the pervading nonsense, cynicism, credulity, speakeasy wit, passion for debunkery, sex-craziness, and music-hall pornography of the times."

"Shipwreck"

"Peaches"

There were other stories, tailor-made for the twenties: the saga of Shipwreck Kelly who spent 23 days and 7 hours atop a Baltimore flagpole, the high point of an era of feats of useless endurance—dance marathons, bunion derbies, rocking chair derbies; the ordeal of Floyd Collins, an unfortunate spelunker trapped in a Kentucky cavern whose agony is turned into a front-page carnival until his death after 17 tortured days; the court-martial of the quick-tempered, farseeing General Billy Mitchell and the marital tribulations of an elderly wolf named Daddy Browning and his plump teen-age bride "Peaches."

Floyd Collins

Big Bill

I'm all alone in a Palace of Stone,
Down in the City of Tears.
Trying to care for an old millionaire,
Wasting the best of my years.

Elsewhere on the front page Mayor "Big Bill" Thompson of Chicago, he who rolls out the red carpet for Capone (a practical gesture since any telltale stains won't show) and rides into office on the promise of a wide-open town and "ten thousand more places than were ever here before," finally draws the line. "If King George comes to Chicago," His Honor says courageously, "I'll crack him in the snoot."

King George stays at home, but his son and heir David, Prince of Wales, England's most popular legal export, ignores the threat and sweeps America off its feet.

HERE HE IS, GIRLS—THE MOST ELIGIBLE BACH-
ELOR YET UNCAUGHT

OH! WHO'LL ASK H.R.H. WHAT HE WEARS
ASLEEP?

PRINCE OF WALES HAS 'EM GUESSING IN THE
WEE HOURS!

Like a bouquet the country offers Prince Charming its most coveted possessions—its headlines and its maidens. Every debutante's mother holds this truth to be self-evident: all men may be created equal but for a son-in-law, give me a prince any day in the week. Not all debutantes concur. One of the brightest of the recent crop, Miss Ellin Mackay, plays hostess to the prince and enlists royalty to stand by while she makes a surreptitious phone call to the prince of Tin Pan Alley, Irving Berlin. David accommodates and within a few months the decade enjoys its most popular marriage, and the Alley, again ready with an appropriate song, obliges with "When a Kid Who Came from the East Side Found a Sweet Society Rose." David hunts American foxes, rides in American parades, starts a

The most eligible
bachelor yet

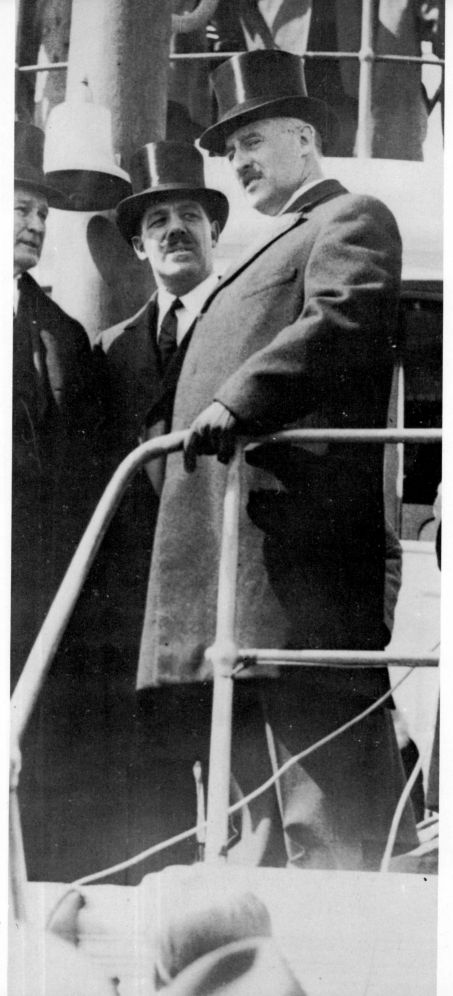

*Grover Whalen
(second from right)
at work*

*Queen Marie
at Columbia . . .*

. . . and at the White House

rage for maroon ties and carnations and goes home to ponder the attractions of American womanhood.

There is a royal something for the boys, too. Marie Alexandra Victoria, Duchess of Saxe, Duchess Royal of Coburg-Gotha, Princess of Hohenzollern, Sigmaringen, Princess Royal of Great Britain and Ireland, and last but not least Queen of Roumania. A regal and mature blonde who resembles something Groucho Marx might pursue across the stage in *Animal Crackers*, Queen Marie arrives from the faraway Balkans for a command coast-to-coast performance, complete with press agent, business manager and a contract with a newspaper syndicate to record her reactions to such quaint native customs as baseball, hot dogs, and apple pie. She drives a locomotive 50 miles an hour, writes an ad for Pond's Cold Cream, confesses her weakness for Western novels, inquires eagerly about our cowboys and Indians, and after traveling 10,000 miles says she hasn't seen half enough of America. "Gracious, tactful and good to look upon, she admirably meets the test of even a republic's idea of what a queen should be," says a newspaper editorial.

"America is destined to be the last refuge of the highborn," sneers an English journalist from overseas.

Not so fast. For Vera, Countess Cathcart, the culpable party in a British divorce suit, it looks like Ellis Island, handle and all. Moral turpitude. Ridiculous. Is the countess any worse than the fellow who throws the party to welcome her ashore with a long-limbed brunette sitting in a bathtub full of champagne? Although Mr. Earl Carroll, a specialist in female nudity, swears it was only ginger ale, he is fined $2,000 and sentenced to a year and a day in Atlanta for perjuring himself regarding violation of the Volstead Act. There are, after all, limits.

But not too many. There go the Marquis Henri de la Falaise and Prince Serge Mdivani spinning straight through customs turnstiles and on to Hollywood to woo and win two members of local royalty, heavy-lidded movie queens Gloria Swanson and Pola Negri.

Life Is Long and Full of Gladness

While Marie and other aristocratic vagabonds are visiting Park Avenue parlors, Hollywood haciendas, and Ladies' Fortnightly Societies along Main Street, thousands of Americans are turning the tables on Columbus and rediscovering Europe.

There's one foreign entanglement that nobody, who can afford it, objects to—an entanglement with France which usually means Paris—and more people can afford it than ever before. The great rush of innocents abroad is on. So it's

> Pack up all my cares and woe
> Here I go
> Singin' low
> Bye, Bye blackbird.

On the *Ile de France* . . . the *Mauretania* . . . the *Aquitania* . . . the *Majestic* . . . shuffleboard and skeet shooting —brisk walks around the deck in plus fours—caviar on the house and no prohibition agents to interrupt the flow of

"Pack up all my cares and woe"

Scotch—really the real stuff. Half a million Americans a year head for the promised land. Some go in search of something—"The most moving and pathetic fact in the social life of America today is emotional and aesthetic starvation. And what is the remedy? Streaming up the longest gangplank in the world . . . a great migration eastward into new prairies of the mind." Some go to escape from something—"There is in America not a trace of that really dignified richness which makes for peasants, household gods, traditions. America has become the wonder of the world simply because America is the purest concentration point for the vices and vulgarities of the world."

But most go just for the fun of it. And why not? Doesn't President Coolidge say that everyone can "regard the present with satisfaction and anticipate the future with optimism"? And doesn't Henry Ford agree that "ninety per cent of the people are satisfied"?

The City of Light

Will Rogers takes exception. "I think Mr. Ford is wrong. . . . It's just got so that ninety per cent of the people in this country don't give a damn." Mr. Rogers also takes a dim view of his foot-loose compatriots—"Half-wits who think that a summer not spent among the decay and mortification of the Old World is a summer squandered." But Will goes too.

Cherbourg . . . or Le Havre. Not everybody on the incoming ships can pronounce the names of these ports but everybody knows that they are somewhere in France and that after a *mauvais quart d'heure* in customs and a little longer on a funny old boat train with a shrill girlish whistle, they will end up in Paris, the city of light, the capital of the world. The intrepid explorers from South Bend and Sacramento are surprised to find the natives are all foreigners, but this is offset by the fact that there are twenty-five francs' worth of French money in every single dollar.

And everybody is here spending it, including the most famous foreign traveler of the times, Lorelei Lee, the blondest of the blondes whom gentlemen are supposed to prefer. Lorelei may not know a word of French but she doesn't

"90% of the people don't give a damn"

Anita Loos

*Worth,
Chanel,
and Cartier*

134

need to. "The way to see America," says a cynic, "is to get a chair at the Café de la Paix." And what would a Frenchman be doing at the Ritz?

Our girl Lorelei Lee has about as deep an appreciation of the glories of Paris as anyone. As she says, "When a girl walks around and reads all of the signs with all of the famous historical names—it really makes you hold your breath." It is not the Louvre, or Notre Dame, or the Conciergerie to which our girl is referring, but the even more resonant names of Worth, Chanel, Cartier. Twenty-five francs to a dollar? Parisian jewelers and couturiers are more than willing to explain the facts of international exchange to Lorelei and her friends.

F. Scott Fitzgerald

All American Rover Girls are not blond and dumb. The typical American miss abroad, says one curbside commentator, is "clad in a minimum of clothing, all cut in the most beautiful style . . . with shingled hair and an air of independence and *savoir-faire* sufficiently strong to rout whole regiments of Roman noblesse . . . a steel-clad Diana, the confusion of European men, who cannot fathom the manners of a demimondaine in the body of an Artemis."

To judge from the society pages of the Main Street *Gazette*, more people are going to Paris than to Okoboji or Yellowstone. To judge from Main Street's living rooms, wormy French provincial or moth-eaten Louis Quinze are better than sturdy Grand Rapids Colonial. "They do things better in Europe," say the conquering heroes, tossing their salads and flipping their crêpes suzettes with a superior air. A half billion dollars poured into the French economy? It's worth every sou.

"By 1928," says a disgruntled F. Scott Fitzgerald, "Paris had grown suffocating. With each new shipment of Amer-

Folies Bergère
FOLIES-BERGERE
Le Rat Mort
MOULIN ROUGE
MOULIN ROUGE CINEMA
ENTREE
BAL
du
Moulin Rouge
UADRILLE
FRENCH CANCAN
ENTREE

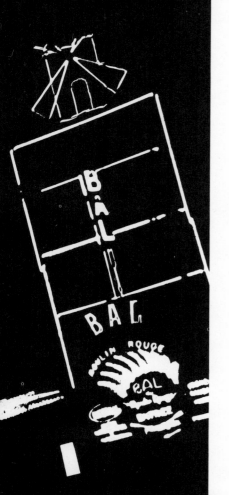

Main Street was never like this

*There **is more** than one Paris*

142

icans spewed up by the boom the quality fell off, until toward the end there was something sinister about the crazy boatloads. They were no longer the simple pa and ma and son and daughter, infinitely superior in their qualities of kindness and curiosity to the corresponding class in Europe, but fantastic neanderthals who believed something, something vague, that you remembered from a very cheap novel. ... There were citizens traveling in luxury in 1928 and 1929 who, in the distortion of their new condition, had the human value of Pekinese, bivalves, cretins, goats."

Well, if not oysters and goats—elephants and ants. As one philosopher of the day puts it:

"Life is short and full of sadness,"
Sighed the dizzy little ant.
"Life is long and full of gladness,"
Cried the jolly elephant.

Either way, off they creep and charge to Montmartre where a fool and his francs are soon parted, off to the *Folies Bergères* where Josephine Baker, a St. Louis girl, shaking a girdle of bananas and singing in a clarinet marmalade voice, does her best for Franco-American understanding. Who said Americans are not interested in foreign affairs? Main Street was never like this. Declare a moratorium on maturity. Why grow up? When you have such a playground.

There is more than one Paris—there are many. While the average American takes a holiday from thinking, others in flight from the society of Messrs Babbitt and Capone think harder than ever before.

"I am wondering just how and where a man of moderate means who prefers simple living, simple pleasures and the things of the mind is going to be able to live any longer in his native country?" muses historian James Truslow Adams.

"As an artist, a man has no home but Paris," comes the enthusiastic reply.

Montparnasse—no mountain, hardly even a hill—is the thinker's stamping ground. The Left Bank, cheaper, less frivolous, and more artistic than the other side of the Seine, opens its garrets and small hotels to the boys and girls who have adopted Paris as their spiritual home. "How you gonna keep them down on the farm?" The answer is, you don't. All roads lead back to Paris for the creatively inclined.

"When you're in Galesburg, Illinois, you want to get to Chicago; then when you get to Chicago, you want to make good in New York. Then when you do put it over in New York, what in God's name have you got? the thoroughly depressing companionship of a lot of other poor small-towners like yourself who don't know what the hell to do with themselves either! . . . You think it would be better in Paris, but then when you get to Paris, you find the same old fizzed-out people and you decide that they're worse than the ones at home because they haven't got even their small-town background to make fools of themselves against." It's a character in a play by Edmund Wilson who speaks for all the sad young men and hopeful dilettantes who have a year in Paris to write their novel or paint their masterpiece, then back to Galesburg, the high school sweetheart and the family store.

Among those who stay on is F. Scott Fitzgerald of St. Paul, Minnesota, who in Paris and the south of France spins his pro-youth, pro-freedom tales of flappers and bootleggers, and with his pretty wife Zelda acts to the hilt the part of one of his own benighted characters. St. Raphaël, Hyères, Fréjus, Plage, Nice, Cannes, Monte Carlo, Antibes, are pounced upon with suicidal gaiety. The great *The Great Gatsby* somehow gets written. Fizzed out? Not quite yet.

Ernest Hemingway, "an extraordinarily good-looking young man, 23 years old . . . with passionately interested, rather than interesting, eyes," arrives from Oak Park, Illinois, and stays to write *The Sun Also Rises*, a novel of Paris and its suburbs over the Pyrenees. "You're an expatriate. You've lost your touch with the soil," he has the book's hero say without a spark of gratitude. "You get precious. Fake European standards have ruined you. You drink yourself to death. You become obsessed by sex. You spend all your time talking, not working. You are an expatriate, see? You hang around cafés. . . . Nobody that ever left their own country ever wrote anything worth printing."

But, contradicts novelist Louis Bromfield, an Ohio boy, "From the vantage point of a Paris café a writer can often see America more clearly. . . . Looking at it from a pinnacle in the midst of a continent that is certainly sick and weary, I have discovered things I could never have noticed in the midst of an Iowa cornfield or in the soda-fountain-bound crowds of Fifth Avenue and Forty-second Street." It's only in Paris that Glenway Westcott can bear to write of his native Wisconsin.

"You are all a lost generation," says lion-headed Gertrude Stein from her café table at the Dôme or her sitting room at 27 rue de Fleurus where she had been pontificating

Gertrude Stein

when the new arrivals were still in knee pants. The Picassos and Cézannes and Matisses bought at bargain prices that hang on her walls give her pronouncements an added awe.

"It was lost," a charter member Malcolm Cowley hastens to agree, "first of all, because it was uprooted, schooled away and almost wrenched away from its attachment to any region or tradition. It was lost because its training had prepared it for another world than existed after the war (and because the war prepared it only for travel and excitement). It was lost because it tried to live in exile. It was lost because it accepted no older guides to conduct and because it had formed a false picture of society and the writer's place in it."

Ezra Pound, who comes to Paris from Idaho by way of

London, wears wide-brimmed hats, velvet jackets, and plays the harpsichord, tells them why they are there. "Paris is the laboratory of ideas; it is there that poisons can be tested, and new modes of sanity be discovered. It is there that the antiseptic conditions of the laboratory exist. That is the function of Paris."

"Pound is a village explainer," snaps Miss Stein, jealous of her prerogatives as the "lost" ones' cicerone, "excellent if you are a village, but if you are not, not."

"The Parisites," as dogs-in-the-manger back home label them, bicker and drink too much and misbehave but they get things done. A dozen little magazines with provocative names—*Broom, Contact, Secession, Gargoyle, Transition, The Transatlantic Review*—come off the presses. Publishing houses spring up to accommodate their creations—Contact Press, Obelisk Press, the Black Sun Press, Three Mountains Press, Hours Press. Pages printed in Paris are

Ezra Pound

packed with the big names of the future—Hemingway, Cummings, William Carlos Williams, Faulkner, Katherine Anne Porter, Eliot, Joyce, Dos Passos, Wilder. Their slogans don't encourage a wide readership—"the writer expresses, does not communicate," "making no compromise with the public taste," "the plain reader be damned." But they work hard and life for them in the unhurried, unstandardized, unmechanized city on the Seine is richly rewarding.

Which doesn't mean that the stay-at-homes are any less busy. America's own Left Bank in Greenwich Village might be a little passé and overpriced but it still boasts a rich selection of poets and peasants. Maxwell Bodenheim, author of the scandalous *Replenishing Jessica,* whose private life —two ladies, suicides for love of him within a few months— is even more scandalous; Hart Crane, Djuna Barnes, Gilbert Seldes.

Don Marquis writes:

> There's a grand poetical "boom" they say,
> (Climb on it, chime on it, brothers of mine!)
> Twixt the dawn and the dusk of each lyrical day
> There's another school started, and all of 'em pay.

Elinor Wylie, e. e. cummings, Robert Frost, Conrad Aiken, Archibald MacLeish, Stephen Vincent Benét, chime in and some of them actually make a living at it.

There are poetic extremes. The ultraclever Dorothy Parker, who finds wit in the most forbidding subjects:

> Razors pain you;
> Rivers are damp;
> Acids stain you;
> And drugs cause cramp.
> Guns aren't lawful;
> Nooses give;
> Gas smells awful;
> You might as well live.

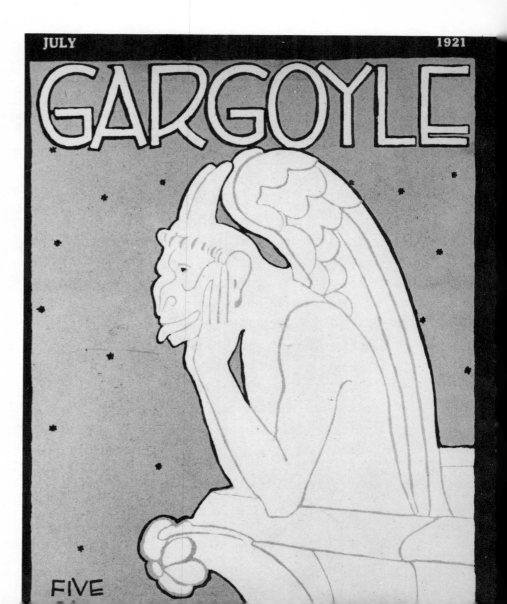

149

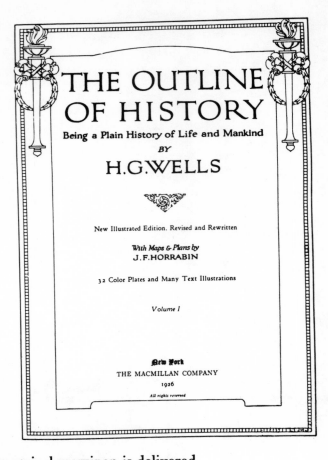

THE OUTLINE
OF HISTORY
Being a Plain History of Life and Mankind
BY
H.G.WELLS

New Illustrated Edition. Revised and Rewritten

With Maps & Plans by
J. F. HORRABIN

32 Color Plates and Many Text Illustrations

Volume I

New York
THE MACMILLAN COMPANY
1926

And Edgar Guest, whose metrical marzipan is delivered to Main Street in wholesale lots:

> God won't ask you if you were clever,
> For I think he'll little care,
> When your toil is done forever
> He may question: "Were you square?"

Edna St. Vincent Millay, redheaded and irresistible, sings her siren songs in the Village for a while, then retires to a mountain top in the Berkshires. But her voice is heard sweet and clear through the decade.

Fiction booms too. *Jurgen, The Private Life of Helen of Troy, The Bridge of San Luis Rey, Death Comes for the Archbishop, An American Tragedy*; and from the South, the *louche*, dysgenic world of Faulkner.

There is a vogue for Outlines, sprawling volumes that take all knowledge as their province. *Outline of History,*

The Outline of Science, The Story of Philosophy, The Story of Mankind. There is even a new club, the Book-of-the-Month Club, to keep all the printed matter circulating.

At home H. L. Mencken, who has made a career of insults and irascibility, calls on the supercilious George Jean Nathan to help him start his own little magazine, *The American Mercury*, and the "booboisie" obligingly subscribes.

> Mencken and Nathan and God;
> Yes, probably, possibly, God.

is a contemporary estimate of this toplofty editorial team.

"If you find so much that is unworthy of reverence in the United States, then why do you live here?" Mr. Mencken asks himself the question that has doubtless occurred to thousands of his long-suffering compatriots. "Why do men go to zoos?" is Mr. Mencken's intransigent reply.

Fully as sparkling as any conversation at a Montparnasse

George Jean Nathan

café is that of the Round Table at the Hotel Algonquin, where "repulsive" and "disgusting" are terms of endearment and Alexander Woollcott, Charles MacArthur, Franklin P. Adams, Robert Benchley, Moss Hart, George Kaufman, Heywood Broun, Harold Ross, Robert Emmet

Eugene O'Neill

Sherwood, Edna Ferber and Dorothy Parker let each other's blood with no pause for transfusions. "A competent old horror with a style that combined clear treacle and pure black bile," is one admirer's thumbnail portrait of ringleader Woollcott. In this mustard-gas atmosphere Miss Parker and Mr. Benchley are encouraged to hire an office and form a corporation for the primary purpose of establishing the cable address PARK BENCH. But it isn't all talk and hilarious make-believe. In between the parry and the lunge of luncheons there are *Vanity Fair*, *Life* and the *New Yorker* to be gotten out: hit plays and best sellers to be written; humor and sentiment to be put down for posterity. *So Big*, *Big Blonde*, *Beggar on Horseback*, *Once in a Lifetime*, *Enough Rope*, *The Front Page*, *The Road to Rome*, an auspicious beginning for a brand-new playwright, Robert Sherwood.

"Wide open as a virgin continent, and as teeming with chances for adventure and fortune" are Sherwood's words for the American theater in the twenties. Among the adventurers are Sherwood himself, Maxwell Anderson, Sidney Howard, Marc Connelly, George S. Kaufman, Elmer Rice. The Bunyan of them all is a smoldering-eyed taciturn Irishman named Eugene O'Neill, an ex-seaman whose first brief one-acters are unveiled to New York audiences in a converted Greenwich Village stable. By the end of the decade O'Neill's steaming dramas have won him two Pulitzer Prizes, stunned restless Broadway audiences into sitting for six-hour stretches through grim, depressing psychological epics.

For those who "go to the theater to be entertained," there are an apparently endless series of *Follies*, *Scandals*,

153

Flo Ziegfeld and friends

Vanities and *Music Box Revues* filled with bare shoulders, bare legs and blackouts.

The stars: there are a whole new galaxy of them— young, dashing, dazzling. Marilyn Miller in *Sally*, then *Sunny;* Jeanne Eagles in *Rain* and *The Letter*. John Barrymore as Hamlet. Helen Hayes in *Coquette* and Katharine Cornell in *The Green Hat*. The Lunts. The Astaires. Fred Allen in *The Little Show*.

And what is the hit of the decade? A starless play greeted with hoots and snorts by the critics, maudlin, inept, ridiculous, with a cast of characters that would never qualify for the Ku Klux Klan let alone the Middletown Country Club —*Abie's Irish Rose*.

Fannie Brice in the "Follies"

Marilyn Miller

"Abie's Irish Rose"

S-18

We

The biggest entertainment of the decade, it so happens, is another transatlantic crossing—made not via first class by tipsy Philistines or via tourist by irate intellectuals, but in a silver monoplane by a clean-living, hundred-per-cent American boy, Charles Augustus Lindbergh. In an age of prodigies he will attempt what no man has ever dared: he will attempt to fly the Atlantic nonstop—New York to Paris—alone. All alone.

Lindbergh, a Midwesterner raised not far from the scene of Sinclair Lewis's much maligned *Main Street*, is one of many pilots, including Richard E. Byrd, who all of a sudden are after a $25,000 prize offered by hotel owner Raymond Orteig eight years before. But it is the twenty-five-

Charles Augustus Lindbergh

"We" are ready

year-old, unknown stunt flyer, wing walker, and mail pilot who moves first. He makes his decision one night while flying the mail, and in six months' time he and his plane *The Spirit of St. Louis* (the partnership Lindy calls "We") are ready. With four sandwiches and three letters of introduction, WE, alone, take off from soggy Roosevelt Field on this dismal morning, May 20, 1927. The time: 7:52 A.M. The goal: Paris.

But Paris is three thousand, six hundred and ten miles away. Suddenly, throughout the world, there is only one story: Lindbergh. THE BIGGEST STORY OF A DECADE, scream headlines. Lindbergh. One single emotion sweeps the United States. One hundred and twenty million people merge their hopes, their prayers, their aspirations, for a lone boy challenging hostile, limitless space.

The ordeal begins. The Lone Eagle, flying the Great Circle course, heads out toward the uncharted void above open seas where none before has ventured alone and lived. "I passed over a tractor by about fifteen feet and a telephone line by about twenty . . . I turned slightly to the right to avoid some high trees on a hill directly ahead." Cape Cod . . . Nova Scotia. Off Newfoundland, darkness and a thin low fog set in. Hour by hour the world below

waits and waits and waits. Storms and worse—sleet. WE have no heat, no radio, no lights, few instruments. Should WE turn back? The weather behind is as bad as the weather in front. Lindbergh goes on.

*The watching
and the waiting*

"We" are alone

Sometimes WE fly at ten thousand feet; sometimes it is only ten, judging wind and drift by foam blown from the whitecaps. Tree-lined shores appear but they are only mirages. WE are still in mid-Atlantic. Hour after hour after hour. At home there is only one concern: Lindbergh. The French, remembering their own fliers Nungesser and Coli —lost over the Atlantic only a few days before—fear for Lindbergh. "All alone, he has no chance."

But as they are saying it, sadly shrugging their shoulders, the tiny silver monoplane is dipping to within a few feet of a fishing boat. "Which way is Ireland?" shouts the pilot.

From the amazed fishermen there is no reply. Didn't they hear? Didn't they understand plain English? The first Europeans to sight Lindy disappear beyond the Atlantic swell, and Ireland rises from the mist ahead.

Next, England. The boy from the farm belt is impressed with the English farms. "Extremely small and unusually neat and tidy," he remarks. Next, France—the lights of Paris, a circling of the Eiffel Tower and the lights of Le Bourget. Can they be so close? After 3,610 miles, it doesn't seem possible. The young pilot goes on for an extra four or five miles, returns and circles in.

"The greatest torrent of mass emotion ever witnessed in human history" begins.

"Perhaps the world was ripe for a youth with a winning smile to flash across its horizon and by the brilliance of his achievement momentarily to dim the ugliness of routine business, politics and crime." Whatever it is, Paris opens its arms. War debts are forgotten. For thirty minutes the milling crowd doesn't let the lanky airman's feet touch the

Triumph

ground. And after that they are placed on the tallest pedestal of the twenties.

Did you hear that his first request was to call his widowed mother, a schoolteacher back in Detroit? Would one of F. Scott Fitzgerald's sad young men do that? Would a bull-baiting Hemingway he-man? Not on your life. That's our Lindy. Lucky Lindy. One in a million.

The President of the French Republic pins the Cross of the Legion of Honor on the lapel of Lindy's borrowed suit. "Lindbergh brought you the spirit of America in a manner in which it could never be brought in a diplomatic sack," says U.S. Ambassador to France, Myron T. Herrick. In Brussels and London it is more of the same.

The cruiser *Memphis* is dispatched to bring Lindbergh home. In Washington the crowd is held at bay by marine bayonets—for a while. Silent Cal waxes eloquent for thirty of the most fullsome paragraphs of his inarticulate career in praise of "this wholesome, earnest, fearless, courageous product of America."

In New York it is still more of the same. A wild welcome by hundreds of boats and small craft and hovering airplanes in New York harbor. Along Broadway, 1,800 tons of ticker tape and confetti (there were only 155 tons for the Armistice). It costs New York $16,000 and takes 2,000 white wings and their brooms to clean up the mess.

For the returning Colonel Lindbergh there is a mail call of two million letters, 100,000 telegrams of congratulations, 14,000 presents, and thousands of proposals of marriage. Offers roll in from the movies, vaudeville, night clubs. If Lindy would get married and let them film it, they'd give him a flat million, and he could choose the lucky girl himself. A tone poem entitled "We" is performed at Lewisohn Stadium and there are a dozen commemorative Tin Pan Alley ditties including one by George M. Cohan himself:

Oh say what a day when Lindy comes home,
When Lindy comes home to his mother . . .
Oh! Say what a day from Gotham to Nome,

Back in England—more of the same

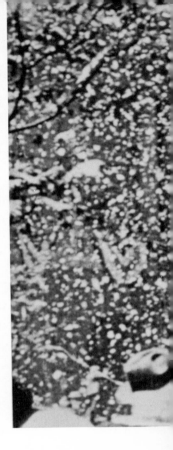

When Lindy comes back from across the foam,
To his Home Sweet Home.

"He has driven the sensation mongers out of the temples of our thought," eulogizes Charles Evans Hughes. "He has kindled anew the fires on the eight ancient altars of that temple. Where are the stories of crime, of divorce, of the triangles that are never equilateral? For the moment we have forgotten. This is the happiest day, the happiest day of all days for America."

"The great thing Lindbergh demonstrates," says Will Rogers more economically, "is a person can still get the entire front page without murdering anybody."

Money making, whoopee making, troublemaking, take a back seat and the cynical, jaded and sophisticated remember nostalgically their own courageous, idealistic beginnings.

Hit One for Me

Lindbergh is not the only one who rates ticker tape and ballyhoo. It takes much less than his impressive accomplishment to coax Jimmy Walker, the "late mayor" of New York (he seldom arrives at work before noon), out onto the steps of City Hall. A year before Lindbergh there he stood welcoming Gertrude Ederle, a sturdy all-American girl who had won her daddy's consent to bob her hair by swimming the English Channel (19 miles in 14 hours and 31 minutes) covered with olive oil, lanolin, vaseline and lard. "When history records the great crossings, they will speak of Moses crossing the Red Sea, Caesar crossing the Rubicon and Washington crossing the Delaware, but frankly your crossing of the British Channel must take its place alongside of these."

It sounded as though Jimmy had shot his bolt on Trudy. What was there left when instead of 19 miles, 3,610 were involved? Plenty. "Colonel Lindbergh, New York City is yours—I don't give it to you; you won it."

How many times will Mayor Walker give New York and its inhabitants away in the remaining years of the decade? Too often, no doubt. But it isn't for the Jazz Age to question the dapper little Irishman in his natty, made-to-order clothes.

"I have a single regret. I have reached the peak of the hill and must start the journey downward," says Beau James, game to the last, although an investigation of his administration has caused him to make a hasty crossing of his own without bothering to finish up his term. "I have

Beau James

Gertrude Ederle

carried youth right up to the 50-yard mark. I had mine and made the most of it."

That's the spirit, Jimmy. That's the spirit, but why stop at the 50-yard line? Kick youth over the goal posts, bat it out of the park with the rest of us.

The rest of us include a host of towering sports idols. Take Jack Dempsey "the Manassa Mauler" for instance,

The long count

and his successive victims—Jess Willard, the Pottawatomie Giant, Luis Firpo, the Wild Bull of the Pampas, Georges Carpentier, the Orchid Man. Everyone has a pet name, even when he's being battered to a pulp.

Thanks to Dempsey and a genius promoter named Tex Rickard, "the manly art of modified murder" draws gates of $1 million, $2 million and more. Dempsey finally loses his heavyweight title to an ex-AEF boxing champion with a taste for Shakespeare named Gene Tunney.

"As Gene Tunney, the most unusual of all ring types, stands on top of the hill," Grantland Rice writes after his victory, "the crowd at large begins to peer in different directions for the most likely challenger to knock him off."

Tunney fools them. Shortly after a return bout with Dempsey (a gate of $2,600,000; 40 million radio listeners, five dead of excitement), he retires a champion and takes a walking tour of Europe with Pulitzer Prize winner Thornton Wilder instead.

In Bowls, and Stadia, and Fields, and Baseball Parks and Arenas 60 million spectators a year watch a succession of triumphs and disasters with roars of joy and howls of anguish. They even leave their assigned places to join in. Football battle fields become bottle fields with raccoon fur, splintered goal posts, dismembered pompons and tattered pennants flying above the melee. A raw edition of the *Harvard Lampoon* leads to Princeton's breaking off all relations with her ancient rival. In Pennsylvania a free-for-all involves coaches, players, officials, and spectators in the after-game mayhem. Sportswriters reverse their function and try to calm down old grads and undergraduates.

But it is difficult when you have Notre Dame's Four Horsemen, Centre's Praying Colonels, or Illinois' "Galloping Ghost" Red Grange ("the young Lochinvar come out of the West") charging down the field. "To hell with glorious defeats. Give us a few inglorious victories," says an old Yale grad. Football is big business, $50 million a year. And as President Coolidge has said, "The business of Amer-

The Galloping Ghost

Rah, rah, rah!

172

Rockne of Notre Dame

ica is business."

To prove he is in tune with the spirit of the times, the young Lochinvar goes pro, signs a $100,000 Hollywood contract, forgets his college education a year ahead of schedule. "I don't like football well enough to play it for nothin'," is his unanswerable comment.

Well, there are still those interested in the glory. Paavo Nurmi, the world's fastest human, a foreigner, but you've got to give a man credit who can run the mile in 4:10:4. Helen Wills, Little Miss Poker Face, with her eyeshade and her pleated skirt—she may not be able to beat the incomparable Suzanne ("la belle") Lenglen but there isn't anyone else she can't. And Big Bill Tilden, and Robert Tyre Jones, and Man o' War—they still do it just for the fun, hay, or hell of it.

"Do, Do, Do, What You Done, Done, Done, Before, Baby." That's all that is necessary and Babe Ruth, the Sultan of Swat, the Mauling Mandarin, is one man who does, does, does it. Training rules—phooey. When you're raised in a reform school and have knocked around the streets of Baltimore in between stretches you develop strong appetites. So it's 12 hot dogs, 8 bottles of soda pop at one sitting, and the twenties' most colossal and highly publicized bellyache. Babe survives, just barely, to drink stronger stuff, chase the girls, squander his $80,000 annual salary, and stand up Queen Marie of Roumania on the steps of the St. Paul City Hall. "Aw, them foreign dames give me a pain. You keep 'em," is his gracious explanation. An idol with feet of clay up to his knees, the mind of a fifteen-year-old and the face of a truant from an Our Gang comedy. But there are 30 homers in 1919 and 60 in 1927. The Home Run King can do no wrong. "Come on, Babe, hit one for me."

And politics, that's just a big game too. After six years of keeping a firm rein on the White House pantry and letting the rest of the country run on a loose leash, Cool Cal

Sportsman Cal

Little Miss Pokerface

The world's fastest human

"chooses not to run."

The new candidate selected in June, 1928, at Kansas City is Herbert Clark Hoover, engineer, self-made millionaire, Secretary of Commerce in two cabinets. His platform is simple and sweet—more prosperity. "Poverty will be banished from the nation." Two chickens in every pot and two cars in every garage. Prohibition is "a great social and economic experiment, noble in motive and far-reaching in purpose," says Mr. Hoover, wisely neglecting to mention the results.

For the Democrats in Houston, Texas, it is Alfred Emanuel Smith, the Happy Warrior. Four successful terms as governor of New York, a pledge to modify prohibition, a cigar, a brown derby, a peculiar way of saying the word "radio."

Politics is just a game but the referees are looking the other way. Fair play—nertz. Country and town are set at

The Sultan of Swat

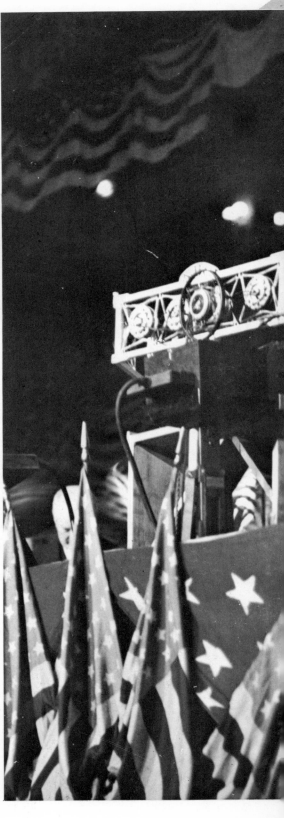

"Two chickens in every pot"

loggerheads. An innocent campaign song, "East Side, West Side, All Around the Town," is interpreted by the Methodist Bishop of Alabama as proof that "Al Smith wants that kind of dirty people that you find today on the sidewalks of New York." City boy Smith is a single generation away from the immigrant, wet as Gertrude Ederle halfway between Cape Griz-Nez and Dover, and Catholic to boot.

"Rum and Romanism," "The Pope will sit in the White House when Hell freezes over." The moribund Ku Klux Klan lifts its ugly head for one last mighty snap. Even with capitalist and bull-market specialist John J. Raskob presiding as Chairman of the Democratic National Committee and assuring everyone that DuPont, General Motors and the Stock Exchange all think Mr. Smith is dandy, it is no go.

"Don't rock the prosperity boat," is the nation's cry. "Who but Hoover?" The round-faced Quaker from the Iowa prairies in his high collar and striped pants sweeps to victory, 444 electoral votes to 87, to become the 31st President of the United States.

"I have no fears for the future of the country. It is bright with hope," says Hoover as he takes over the leadership of the nation from Coolidge. Hoover, inspecting his new quarters, installs a telephone in his office, closes the White House stables, retires the White House yacht and hires five secretaries where only one had been before.

The Happy Warrior

To the Bulls operating on the Stock Exchange, and the country at large, Hoover's victory means "Four more years of prosperity." Will Rogers has a cautioning word for the man he calls "Doctor of Catastrophe": "Nothing short of heaven will we accept under Hoover. Good luck to you, Herb."

182

The New York

"All the News That's
Fit to Print."

Copyright, 1928, by The New

VOL. LXXVIII....No. 25,855.

NEW YORK. WEDNESDA

HOOVER WINS 407 TO
SMITH LOSES STAT
ROOSEVELT IS EL

OVER CARRIES
LINOIS, SWEEPING
N THE STATE TICKET

th Wins in Chicago, but His
epublican Rival Gets Big
Down-State Vote.

"A STRONG FOR HOOVER

raska Puts Republican in
Lead and His Victory
Seems Certain.

HIGAN ALSO REPUBLICAN

ver Sweeps Ohio by a Big
Majority — Entire State
Ticket Elected.

ecial to The New York Times.
ICAGO. Nov. 6.—Illinois went
ublican today. Herbert Hoover
the State ticket, headed by
s L. Emmerson, candidate for
rnor, and Otis F. Glenn, nomi-
for United States Senator, won
uch large figures in down-State
tory that close battles over some
e places in Cook County were
nated.
hough he apparently lost Chi-
to Governor Smith, incomplete
ns indicated that Hoover had

U.S. Senators Elected

REPUBLICAN—18

California	*H. W. Johnson
Connecticut.	‡F. C. Walcott
Delaware..John G. Townsend Jr.	
Idaho	§John Thomas
Illinois	§Otis F. Glenn
Indiana	⸰A. R. Robinson
Maine	¶Frederick Hale
Maryland.	‡P. L. Goldsborough
Michigan	†A. H. Vanderberg
Nebraska.	*Robert B. Howell
New Jersey.	‡Hamilton F. Kean
North Dakota	*Lynn J. Frazier
Ohio	*Simeon D. Fess
Ohio	§T. E. Burton
Pennsylvania	*David A. Reed
Rhode Island.	‡Felix Hebert
Vermont	*Frank L. Greene
Wisconsin..	*R. M. La Follette Jr.

DEMOCRATS—9

Arizona	*Henry F. Ashurst
Florida	*Park Trammell
Massachusetts	*David I. Walsh
Mississippi	*H. D. Stephens
New York	*R. S. Copeland
Tennessee	*Kenneth McKellar
Texas	‡Tom Connally
Utah	*William H. King
Virginia	*C. A. Swanson

FARMER-LABORITE—1

Minnesota	*Henrik Shipstead

IN DOUBT—7

Missouri	New Mexico
Montana	Washington
Nevada	West Virginia
	Wyoming

*Re-elected for full term ending
March 3, 1935.
†Elected for both long and short
terms.
‡Elected for full term ending
March 3, 1935.
¶Re-elected Sept. 10, 1928, for
full term ending March 3, 1935.
§Elected for short term ending
March 3, 1933.

NEW JERSEY GIVES
REPUBLICAN SLATE
A HEAVY MAJORITY

Incomplete Figures for State
Show Hoover Leads Smith
by 116,944.

LARSON AHEAD OF DILL

Victory for Republican by
166,340 Is Indicated in
Gubernatorial Race.

KEAN BEATING EDWARDS

Strong Republican Showing Is a
Damaging Blow to Prestige
of Hague as Leader.

Herbert Hoover's indicated plurality in New Jersey was 309,420 early
this morning when the tabulation of
returns from 1,102 of the 2,920 districts gave Hoover 303,792 and Smith
186,848. In the metropolitan district
of New Jersey the Republican and
Democratic candidates ran a close
race.
In Essex County, which includes
Newark, tabulation of the vote in
150 of the 481 districts showed that
it stood, Hoover, 39,122; Smith, 31,-
810.
Hamilton F. Kean was leading Sen-

Gov. Smith's Messa

Governor Smith sent the
midnight to his successful rival:

*Hon. Herbert Hoover,
Palo Alto, Cal.:*

I congratulate you heartily
you my sincere good wishes for
for the success of your Adminis

Electora

	HOO
Arizona	3
California	13
Colorado	6
Connecticut	7
Delaware	3
Florida	6
Idaho	4
Illinois	29
Indiana	15
Iowa	13
Kansas	10
Kentucky	13
Maine	6
Maryland	8
Michigan	15
Minnesota	12
Missouri	18
Montana	4
Nebraska	8
	SMI
Alabama	12
Arkansas	9

k Times.

LATE EDI
5:30 A. M

WEATHER—Fair today; cloudy

The winner?
Who but Hoover?

Company

MBER 7, 1928.　　TWO CENTS In Greater | THREE (
New York | Within 2·

9; DOUBTFUL 5

ROKE

ERNO

ARRIES NEW YORK BY

n Nominee Captures N
kes Wisconsin; Breaks
, Winning Virginia, Flor

NORTH CAROLINA AND BAY

185

n Belt in Republican Column in R
g Vote—Kentucky, Missouri an
ennessee Lost to Democrats.

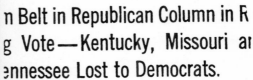

nprecedented numbers, a myriad of American (
Herbert Hoover of California for President of the
es Curtis of Kansas for Vice President.
nced is the victory of these candidates of the Repul
Democratic competitors, Governor Alfred E. Smi
nee for President, and Joseph T. Robinson of Arka
ntial nominee, cannot be determined until the stupen
40,000,000 or more votes is completed, but a Republi
ice at the polls, and it will be reflected in a heavy Hoov
Curtis majority of the 531 ballots in the Electoral College.

400 Electoral Votes for Hoover

Mr. Hoover is assured of more than 400 electoral votes. It is probab
that his majority will increase as further returns are received. He ha
broken the traditionally Democratic Solid South. He has carried Virgini
and returns from Florida indicate that he has won in that State. His tally
in the Electoral College may go as high as 444 votes if North Carolina,
North Dakota and Texas, which are very close, are added to his strength,
or even to the stupendous total of 462, if the count now proceeding in

nia 8
.... 13
.... 3
.... 407
.... 10
nd 5
olina 9

basis of returns from 7,718 election
districts out of the 8,267 in the State.
A plurality of about 40,000 for Mr.
Roosevelt was indicated on these
figures, and '' is possible that this
plurality might be cut somewhat by
the returns from the missing districts but not enough to give Mr.
Ottinger the State.
Senator Royal S. Copeland, candidate for re-election on the Demo-

Boom . . .

Good luck? Who needs it? All you need is a good tip. Luck is like the air—everywhere.

"Good News, that's what we're waiting for."

And it is there every morning in the stock quotations. Americans have become fearless speculators—living in a make-believe world, getting rich quick without working. God owes the middle class a fortune. And not only the middle class.

"Everybody Ought to be Rich," says John J. Raskob in an appropriately democratic article in the *Ladies Home Journal*. All it takes is $15 a month as a starter and with the market on your side you'll have $80,000 in twenty years. Or if that is too long to wait, take $200 of your savings, borrow $300 more and plunge. The water's fine. Even the cool Mr. Coolidge has enthused over the "absolute soundness" of things, and volunteered the judgment that stocks are "cheap at current prices."

The current prices:

A T & T 335
General Electric   396
Montgomery Ward   466
Radio (that word Al Smith can't pronounce) 505

Don't sell America short. Who's selling anything short? Why, man, we've scarcely started. Everything that goes up, has to continue going up.

"Led by these mighty knights of the automobile industry, the steel industry, the radio industry, . . . and finally joined, in despair, by many professional traders who, after much sackcloth and ashes, had caught the vision of progress, the Coolidge market had gone forward like the phalanxes of Cyrus, parasang upon parasang and again parasang upon parasang," says an authority of the day. We don't know what parasangs are but we're all for them. There are other magic words—leverage, investment trusts, holding companies, pools, growth possibilities, margin. What do they mean? It's obvious. Money.

From Boston to San Francisco, to Corpus Christi, the Bull Market is the national mania: the biggest news of the day—every day—coast to coast to coast.

"Is Everybody Happy?" I'll tell the cockeyed world. And the world *is* cockeyed. What difference does it make if you buy a railroad stock called Seaboard Air Line and think it has something to do with flying? It does. Flying high, wide and handsome.

Buy on margin. Brokers' loans are available. All you have to have is five cents for a telephone call and you can even get that on credit.

Everybody's doing it. Doing what? Getting rich. Why not? Hasn't the august Arthur Brisbane said, "If buying and selling stocks is wrong the government should close the Stock Exchange. If not, the Federal Reserve should mind its own business." The Federal Reserve, after a few fluttering motions of apprehension, does mind its own business. And so does President Hoover, who for a moment looked as though he might become a spoilsport.

What is there to spoil anyway? Production, sales, bank deposits, brokers' loans, stocks, especially brokers' loans and stocks, zoom upward.

Greenwich Villagers and repatriated expatriates give up talking about Freud, T. S. Eliot, James Joyce and Gertrude Stein, Picasso and Dada in favor of U.S. Steel and Electric Bond and Share.

Housewives are more interested in the price of Radio than the price of Roast Beef. Waitresses and men's room attendants in fashionable clubs, gardeners with an opportunity to loiter behind hedges on Long Island estates, taxi drivers, charwomen, anyone who can snoop, peep or eavesdrop, has a tip. We have all heard about the chauffeur who has made a killing and retired to a country estate. Now *his* chauffeur is doing it. If you think Cheops' pyramid is something, just observe the activities of a firm called Goldman, Sachs and Company.

"Good news, that's what we're waiting for"

189

It is standing room only in the brokerage houses. The hinterlands have sprouted their own cunning little stock exchanges to accommodate the Wall Street overflow.

"There has been an interlude of uncertainty and inconvenience for speculators crossing the ocean," investment counselors admit; but this unfortunate situation is corrected and tapes are ticking aboard the *Leviathan* and *Ile de France* to inform passengers of the additional money they'll have to squander when they reach the other side. For the convenience of those remaining at home, Western Union has announced that it plans to spend $4 million to increase the rate of stock-tickers from a desultory 300 to 500 characters a minute.

> Birds do it, Bees do it.
> Even educated fleas do it.
> Let's do it.

Four million shares a day, five million, six, seven, that's nothing. "Nothing can arrest the upward movement," say the oracles. The Secretary of the Treasury predicts, "The

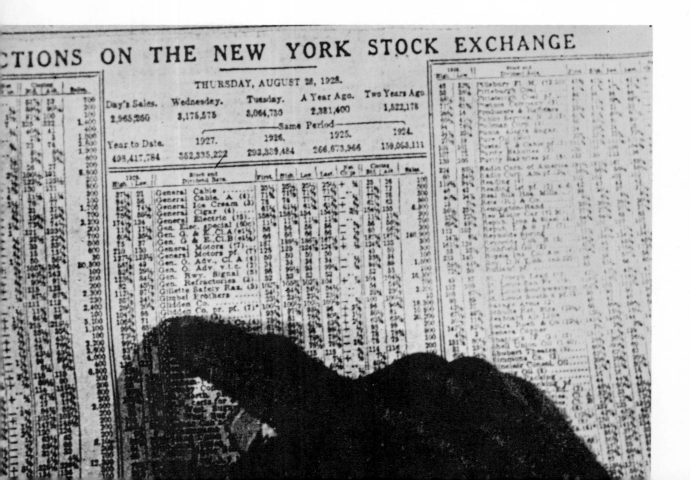

high tide of prosperity will continue."

Even New York's sky line is rising in empathy. Multi-millionaire ex-railroad apprentice Walter P. Chrysler is building his own 68-story skyscraper with an elevator that can rise 1,000 feet in 60 seconds. No matter that the building is only going to be 800 feet high.

Nor that three hundred million shares are being carried on margin and brokers' loans are at an all-time high. Don't worry, the values are there—somewhere. The market is not only selling common and preferred stocks in the future. They have invaded the hereafter. Mr. Chrysler's elevators will have company.

Everything is the flea's eyebrows . . . the snake's hips . . . and I don't mean maybe.

Boom on Wall Street—Bonanza on Park Avenue and Sunset Boulevard. For $30,000 you can get a Budd automobile, Cleopatra green with a velvet and broadcloth interior and arm rests upholstered in hand-tooled Venetian leather.

Black, Starr and Frost have just put together the finest pearl necklace in existence and have taken a two-page ad in the *New Yorker* to launch it—price for the incomparable single strand of 59 pearls with a diamond baguette thrown in, just $685,000. Expensive? Well, hasn't Mr. Andrew Mellon, the Secretary of the Treasury, just paid $970,000 for some painting by Raphael that isn't even new? Mr. J. P. Morgan is giving away his yacht. Retrenchment? Nonsense. He has a bigger and better one on order. John Barrymore has three swimming pools at his "Chinese tenement" in the Beverly Hills and a genuine Old English taproom in the basement. Marion Davies has only two pools but she sets up a merry-go-round on her tennis courts to entertain the guests who haven't room to get wet.

Things are lively in Florida, too. Mrs. Edward Hutton whose fortune comes from, among other things, Grape Nuts and Post Toasties, has hired Ringling Brothers' circus to amuse her guests at Mar-A-Lago, her Spanish-type castle in Palm Beach.

"Mabel," Mr. A. Atwater Kent, who manufactures

radios and specializes in $50,000 parties, says sternly to his wife, "you aren't spending enough money."

In good old New York there is a second House of Morgan, open till the small hours with Helen on the piano. There is Villa Vallee with Rudy manning the megaphone; and Texas Guinan, "the beautiful cactus flower who became a Broadway orchid," may be a bit wilted on the outer petals but she still is all over the place shouting "Hello Sucker" as she stirs up a pungent midnight goulash of the underworld, big butter-and-egg men and high society. The recently redecorated Central Park Casino is "the most expensive restaurant in America": $3 for a bottle of soda, and $200 tips for the hat-check girl—if you are Jimmy Walker.

Is Main Street's nose out of joint over all the high stepping in the big city? Not on your life buoy. Six billion dollars of installment buying have livened things up there too. If you don't want to buy, ads will convince you that you should. If you don't have it—pink toothbrush, lordosis backline, halitosis, B.O., athletes foot, and etiquette—ads will make you wonder if you shouldn't. And once you have, tell you how to get rid of it. If you occasionally get out of your element in the social turmoil—there is a sure solution. "Be nonchalant, light a Murad." Ads bad? Haven't George B. Shaw, H. G. Wells and Henry Ford all been featured recently in blurbs for Simmons Beauty Rest Mattresses?

Of course there are a few spoilsports. Senator Carter Glass refers to the stock market with an uncomplimentary adjective—"frantic." Some people object when after seven years of slow torture Sacco and Vanzetti are finally electrocuted in Charlestown. But America has shown its heart is in the right place. Didn't the Arkansas State Senate formally adopt a resolution demanding the release of handsome young Tom Carr of The Gumps from prison when he is falsely convicted of stealing $10,000? And doesn't softhearted comic strip artist Sidney Smith spring him with a few deft strokes of the pen when the public outcry becomes unbearable?

The second House of Morgan

What does William Allen White mean when he says, "What a sordid decade is passing! The spirit of our democracy has turned away from the things of the spirit, got its share of its patrimony ruthlessly, and has gone out and lived riotously and ended up by feeding it to the swine. . . . We sit in our offices and do unimportant things and go home at night and think unimportant thoughts"?

Hasn't he heard Eddie Cantor's new song—"Another season, another reason for making whoopee"? Eddie is in the market too. Even a comedian can make a killing. He's just announced he's going to retire. But there is still time for one last flyer. Or is there?

September, 1929. The soaring stocks hit something. The ceiling? No. "A permanently high plateau." That's more like it with more Himalayas there in the distance. Now, here's a tip—some of these prices will look ridiculously low in a year or two. Remember the dip in June. Look what happened. The Bull came back pawing the ground.

True, Bernard Baruch, the most spectacular speculator of them all, has begun unloading stocks and buying bonds. But then he advises "to sell to the sleeping point—the point where you can sleep without worrying." Who's worrying,

"Hello, Sucker!"

195

Making whoopee

and who wants to sleep? Who can sleep? The weather is awful. Ninety-four degrees on the sidewalk outside the Stock Exchange. But inside, the market is fine. Sure, there are "technical readjustments" once in a while as "the lunatic fringe of margin speculators is being shaken out." But "conditions are fundamentally sound. . . . Nothing can arrest the upward movement."

October—Indian Summer—1929. The weather has improved but the market hasn't. The lunatic fringe has raveled back into the fabric. "A little distress selling, fundamentally sound, organized support."

S-T-E-A-D-Y Everybody! *Calm thinking is in order. Heed the words of America's greatest bankers*, reads an ad in the *Wall Street Journal*. But America's greatest bankers cannot stop the unraveling.

In the decade of bad taste, in the revolution of manners and morals, the Bears finally jump the Bulls. Down go the common stocks—down, down, down. Tuesday, October 29, 1929; in history's worst panic over sixteen million shares are dumped on the market. Over fourteen billion dollars goes with them and along with it the fever dreams of a whole nation.

A T & T —205
General Electric —223
Montgomery Ward —53¾
Radio —36½

On the big boards above the Stock Exchange the handwriting appears. But it is too late. "Wall Street Lays an Egg." And so do the Twenties.

"The greatest, gaudiest spree in history" is at an end. The Jazz Age is over, all over.

196

197

Bibliography

Allen, Frederick Lewis, *Only Yesterday*. New York and London, Harper & Bros., 1931.

Cowley, Malcolm, *Exile's Return*. New York, W. W. Norton & Co., Inc., 1934.

Ewen, David, *Panorama of American Popular Music*. Englewood Cliffs, N. J., Prentice-Hall, 1957.

Fitzgerald, F. Scott, *The Crack-Up*, ed. by Edmund Wilson. New York, J. Laughlin, 1945.

Fowler, Gene, *Beau James*. New York, Viking Press, 1949.

Galbraith, John Kenneth, *The Great Crash*. Boston, Houghton-Mifflin, 1955.

Green, Abel and Laurie, Joe Jr., *Show Biz*. New York, Henry Holt & Co., 1951.

Hoffman, Frederick, *The Twenties*. New York, Viking Press, 1955.

Johnston, Charles H. L., *Famous American Athletes of Today*. Boston, L. C. Page & Co., 1928.

Leighton, Isabel, ed., *The Aspirin Age 1919-1941*. New York, Simon & Shuster, 1949.

Lindbergh, Charles, *We*. New York and London, G. P. Putnam's Sons (The Knickerbocker Press), 1927.

Lynd, Robert S., and Lynd, Helen Merrell, *Middletown*. New York, Harcourt Brace & Co., 1929.

Mencken, H. L., *The Vintage Mencken*, ed. by Alistair Cooke. New York, Vintage Books, 1955.

Mizener, Arthur. *The Far Side of Paradise*. Boston, Houghton-Mifflin, 1951.

Morison, Samuel Eliot, and Commager, Henry Steele, *The Growth of the American Republic*, Vol. II. New York, Oxford University Press, 1956, © 1950.

Morris, Joe Alex, *What A Year!* New York, Harper & Bros., 1956.

Morris, Lloyd, *Not So Long Ago*. New York, Random House, 1949.

Overton, Grant, ed., *Mirrors of the Year*. New York, F. A. Stokes Co., 1927-28.

Robinson, Henry Morton, *The Fantastic Interim*. New York, Harcourt Brace & Company, 1943.

Rogers, Will, *The Autobiography of Will Rogers*, selected and ed. by Donald Day, foreword by Bill and Jim Rogers. Boston, Houghton-Mifflin Co., 1949.

Snyder, Louis L., and Morris, Richard B., editors, *A Treasury of Great Reporting*, preface by Herbert Bayard Swope. New York, Simon & Shuster, 1949.

Spaeth, Sigmund, *A History of Popular Music in America*. New York, Random House, 1948.

Stein, Gertrude, *The Autobiography of Alice B. Toklas*. New York, The Literary Guild, 1933.

Sullivan, Mark, *Our Times; the United States*. New York, C. Scribner's Sons, 1927–35.

Wilson, Edmund, *The American Earthquake*. Garden City, N. Y., Doubleday, 1958.

———, *The Shores of Light*. New York, Farrar, Straus and Young, 1952.

Acknowledgments

The authors wish to thank:

Music Publishers Holding Corporation for permission to quote from "Charleston," by Johnson and McPherson, Copyright 1923 by Harms, Inc., Copyright Renewed, Used by Permission; from "Carolina in the Morning," by Walter Donaldson and Gus Kahn, Copyright 1922 by Jerome H. Remick & Company, Copyright Renewed & Assigned to Remick Music Corporation, Used by Permission; from "Bye Bye Blackbird," by Mat Dixon and Ray Henderson, Copyright 1926 by Jerome H. Remick & Company, Copyright Renewed & Assigned to Remick Music Corporation, Used by Permission; from "Let's Do It," by Cole Porter, Copyright 1928 by Harms, Inc., Copyright Renewed, Used by Permission; from "Do It Again," by George Gershwin, Copyright 1922 by New World Music Corporation, Copyright Renewed, Used by Permission.

Mrs. Norma Millay Ellis for permission to quote from "First Fig," Copyright 1922, 1950 by Edna St. Vincent Millay, from *Collected Poems*, Harper & Brothers.

Leo Feist Inc., Music Publishers for permission to quote from "Sleepy Time Gal," Lyrics by Joseph R. Alden and Raymond B. Egan, Music by Ange Lorenzo and Richard A. Whiting, © 1925/Copyright renewal 1953 Leo Feist Inc., Used by special permission.

Bourne, Inc., Music Publishers for permission to quote from "Yes Sir, That's My Baby," by Walter Donaldson and Gus Kahn, Copyright 1925 by Bourne, Inc., Used By Permission Of The Copyright Owner.

Shapiro, Bernstein & Co. Inc. for permission to quote from "Yes! We Have No Bananas," by Frank Silver and Irving Cohn, Copyright 1923 by Skidmore Music Co. Inc., Copyright renewed.

Fred Fisher Music Company, Inc. for permission to quote from "I'm All Alone In A Palace Of Stone," words and music by Lon Mooney, by permission of the copyright owners.

Doubleday & Company, Inc. for permission to quote from "There's a grand poetical 'boom' they say," by Don Marquis.

The Viking Press, Inc. for permission to quote from "Resumé," by Dorothy Parker, from *The Portable Dorothy Parker*, Copyright 1926, 1944, 1954 by Dorothy Parker.

The photographs on pages 2, 4, 5, 12, 13, 16, 17 (a), 24, 27, 28, 29 (a,b), 31, 32, 33 (a,b,c), 34 (a), 35 (b), 36 (b), 37, 41, 42 (a), 43 (a,b), 45, 46 (a), 48 (a,b), 49, 54, 58 (a,b), 59, 60, 61, 63, 64, 65, 68 (a), 69 (a,b), 70, 71, 76 (c), 79 (b), 80, 82, 85, 86 (a,b), 89 (b), 90, 92, 94, 97 (a), 99, 104 (a,b), 106, 108, 109, 110, 114, 115 (a), 116, 120, 121, 122 (a,b), 127 (b), 129, 131, 134 (a), 146, 147, 153, 154, 155 (a,b), 161, 162, 166 (a), 167, 169, 170, 177, 181, 182, 185, 193(a), 197 (a) are reproduced with the permission of Brown Bros.

The photographs on pages 30 (a,b), 34 (b), 53, 62 (b), 100 (b), 101, 112, 115 (b), 118, 119, 127 (a), 151, 152, 172 (a), 174 (b), 176 (b), 179 are reproduced with the permission of Underwood and Underwood.

Nancy H. Dale for format design.

Index

House of (Helen) Morgan, 192
Howard, Sidney, 153
Hughes, Charles Evans, 15, 28, 165
Hungary, 11
Hupmobile, 71
Hutton, Mrs. Edward, 191
Hyères, 145

I

Ile de France, 130, 190
installment buying, 38, 192
It (by Elinor Glyn), 1
"It" girl, 61
"It Had to Be You," 78
I.W.W., 13

J

James, Beau, 168
"Joe College," 52
Johnson, Hiram W., 5
Jones, Billy, 74
Jones, Robert Tyre, 175
Jordan (automobile), 71
Joyce, James, 148, 189
Joyce, Peggy Hopkins, 109, 110
Jugoslavia, 11
Jung, Carl, 113
Jurgen, 150

K

Kahn, Otto, 38
Kaiser, the, 3
Kaufman, George S., 152, 153
Keaton, Buster, 64
Kelly, Machinegun, 105
Kelly, Shipwreck, 120, 123
Kent, A. Atwater, 191
Kern, Jerome, 81
Keynes, Maynard, 5
Kid, The, 64
King of Kings, The, 61
Kramer, John F., 95
Ku Klux Klan, 16-24, 182

L

Ladies Home Journal, 186
Lady Be Good, 81
La Guardia, Fiorello, 16, 101
La Marr, Barbara, 66
La Rocque, Rod, 56
Larson, John M., 62
Lawrence, Gertrude, 81

Lazarus, Emma, 14
League of Nations, Covenant of, 5, 7
Le Bourget Field, 161
Left Bank, 144
Le Havre, 132
Lenglen, Suzanne, 175
Leopold, Nathan, 112, 113
Letter, The, 154
Leviathan, 190
Lewis, Sinclair, 35, 37, 68, 70, 156
Lewisohn Stadium, 163
Life, 153
Lindbergh, Charles A., 156-165, 168
Lippmann, 16, 33
Little Lord Fauntleroy, 64
"Little Miss Poker Face" (Helen Wills),
    175, 176
Little Shoes, The, 154
Lloyd, Harold, 64, 66
Lodge, Henry Cabot, 5, 7
Loeb, Richard, 112, 113
Lombard, Guy, 78, 83
Longworth, Alice Roosevelt, 28
Loos, Anita, 134
Lopez, Vincent, 78
Lorelei Lee, 132, 136
Lorimer, George Horace, 38
"Lost Generation," 145
Louis XIV, 3
Louis XVI, 3
Lowell, A. L., 15
Lunt, Alfred, 154
Lunts, the (Alfred Lunt and Lynn Fontanne), 154

M

MacArthur, Charles, 152
Mackay, Ellin, 124
MacLeish, Archibald, 148
"Ma—He's Making Eyes at Me," 47
Mah-jong, 44
"Main Street," 35, 37
Majestic, 130
Male and Female, 61
"Manassa Mauler" (Jack Dempsey), 169
Man Nobody Knows, The, 38
Man o' War, 175
Mar-A-Lago, Palm Beach, 191
Marie Antoinette, 3
Marie of Roumania, 127, 128, 130
Marion, Ohio, 26
Mark of Zorro, The, 64
Marquis, Don, 148
Marshall, Thomas R., 11

Marx, Groucho, 128
mass production, 38
Matisse, 146
Mauretania, 130
"Maybe," 81
McPherson, Aimee Semple, 110, 118
McWilliams, Carey, 120
Mdivani, Serge, 128
Means, Gaston, 28, 31
Meighan, Thomas, 56
Mellon, Andrew, 28, 83, 191
Memphis, the, 163
Mencken, Henry L., 28, 34, 44, 45, 116, 151
Merz, Charles, 75
Mespot, the, 4
Metropolitan Opera, 78
Miami Beach, 89, 90
Millay, Edna St. Vincent, 16, 52, 53, 150
Miller, Marilyn, 154, 155
Miller, Thomas W., 28, 31
Mills, Charlotte, 109
Mills, James, 109
Mills, Mrs. Eleanor, 109
Minter, Mary Miles, 66
Mirror, the New York, 109
Mitchell, Billy, 123
Mitchell, Charles E., 88
Mix, Tom, 66
Monte Carlo, 145
Montgomery Ward, 92, 188, 196
Montmartre, 144
Morgan, Helen, 78, 192, 193
Morgan, J. P., 13, 191
Morrow, Dwight, 34
mortgages, 88
Morton, Jelly Roll, 78
musical comedies, 81
Music Box Revue, 154
"My Blue Heaven," 78

N

Nash (automobile), 71
Nathan, George Jean, 151
National City Bank, 88
Negri, Pola, 56, 128
New Orleans, 78
New Yorker, The, 153, 191
Nice, 145
Nilsson, Anna Q., 56
Normand, Mabel, 66
Norris, Kathleen, 44, 45
Notre Dame College, 171
Nungesser, Charles, 160
Nurmi, Paavo, 175, 177

O

O'Bannion, Dion, 105
Obelisk Press, 147
October 1929, 196
O'Donnell, Klondike, 105
Ohio Gang, 26
Oh, Kay, 81
Oliver, King, 71
Once in a Lifetime, 153
O'Neill, Eugene, 152, 153
operettas, 81
"Orchid Man" (Georges Carpentier), 171
Orlando, Vittorio Emanuele, 4, 5, 9
Orteig, Raymond, 156
Ory, Kid, 78
Our Gang Comedy, 175
Outline of History, The, 150, 151

P

Packard automobile, 71
Paige automobile, 71
Palmer, A. Mitchell, 13
Palmer, Olive (the Palmolive girl), 72
Paramount, the, 64
Paris, 3, 5, 132, 144-147, 157, 161
Parker, Dorothy, 148, 152
Parsons, Louella, 66
peacemakers, 4
Pearson, Edmund Lester, 109
Pennsylvania Avenue, Washington, 24, 35
Picasso, 146, 189
"Pickfair," 66
Pickford, Mary, 41, 43, 64
Pierce Arrow, 70, 71
"Pig Woman, the," 109
Plage, 145
Plainfield, Illinois, 24
Poland, 11
Polish Corridor, 4
politics, 178
Porter, Cole, 81
Porter, Katherine Anne, 148
Post Toasties, 191
"Pottawatomie Giant" (Jess Willard), 171
Pound, Ezra, 146, 147
"Praying Colonels," 171
Preface to Morals, A, 33
Prince of Wales, 124, 125
Princeton University, 171
Private Life of Helen of Troy, The, 150
prizefighters, 171
prosperity, 191

Swedish Immanuel Congregational Church, 117
"S' Wonderful," 81

T

Talmadge, Constance, 56
Talmadge, Norma, 56
tariffs, 88
Tashman, Lilyan, 66
Taylor, William Desmond, 66
Tchaikovsky, 72
Teapot Dome scandal, 31
telephone operators strike, 13
Ten Commandments, The, 61
Thayer, Judge Webster, 15
"There'll Be Some Changes Made," 78
Thief of Bagdad, The, 64
This Side of Paradise, 52
Thomas, Olive, 66
Thompson, "Big Bill," 124
Three Mountains Press, 147
"Tiger, the" (Clemenceau), 4
Tilden, Big Bill, 175
Tin Lizzy, 72
Tin Pan Alley, 124, 163
"To a Wild Rose," 47
Torrio, Johnny, 105
Town Hall, 78
Transatlantic Review, The, 147
Transition, 147
Trentino, the, 4
Trieste, 4
"Truth about the Younger Generation, The," 113
Tulsa, Oklahoma, 24
Tunney, Gene, 171
Tyler, Elizabeth, 20

U

union organizers, 15
University of Chicago, 112
U. S. Steel, 189

V

"Vagabond Lover, A," 78
Valentino, Rudolph, 56, 61, 66
Vallee, Rudy, 78, 79
Vanities, 154

Vanity Fair, 113, 153
Van Loon, Hendrik Willem, 151
Vanzetti, Bartolomeo, 15
Versailles, 3, 5, 9
Veterans' Bureau, 3

W

Walker, Jimmy, 168
Wallace, Henry C., 28
Wall Street, 83, 94, 191
Wall Street bomb explosion, 12
Wall Street Journal, 196
Washington, D.C., 5
Way Down East, 64
"We," 163
Weeks, John W., 28
Wells, H. G., 151, 192
Westcott, Glenway, 145
Western Union, 190
Whalen, Grover, 126
White, Alice, 56, 58
White, William Allen, 195
Whiteman, Paul, 77, 78
"Why Was I Born?", 78
"Wild Bull of the Pampas" (Luis Firpo), 171
Wilder, Thornton, 148, 150, 171
Willard, Jess, 171
Williams, William Carlos, 148
Wills, Helen, 175, 176
Willys-Knight Six, 71
Wilson, Edmund, 145
Wilson, Woodrow, 3, 5, 9, 26, 31, 53, 95
Wisconsin, 145
Wolverines, the, 78
Woollcott, Alexander, 152
World War I, 3
Worth, 136
Wylie, Elinor, 148
Wynn, Ed, 76

Y

Yap, Island of, 4
Youmans, Vincent, 81

Z

Ziegfeld, Flo, 153
Ziegfeld Follies, 4, 153